Redford Township District Library
25320 West Six Mile Road
Redford, MI 48240

www.redford.lib.mi.us

Hours:

Mon–Thur 10–8:30
Fri–Sat 10–5
Sunday (School Year) 12–5

39009000054003

D0161758

Eating Right
An Introduction to Human Nutrition

Basic Nutrition

Nutrition and Eating Disorders

Nutrition for Sports and Exercise

Nutrition and Weight Management

Eating Right
An Introduction to Human Nutrition

Nutrition and Eating Disorders

Lori A. Smolin, Ph.D.
Mary B. Grosvenor, M.S., R.D.

Preface: Lori A. Smolin, Ph.D. and
Mary B. Grosvenor, M.S., R.D.

Introduction:
Richard J. Deckelbaum, MD, CM, FRCP(C)
Robert R. Williams Professor of Nutrition
Director, Institute of Human Nutrition
College of Physicians and Surgeons
of Columbia University

CHELSEA HOUSE
P U B L I S H E R S
A Haights Cross Communications Company
Philadelphia

Frontispiece: Many people today are obsessed with their body weight, and may fall victim to dangerous eating disorders. One of the best ways to stay fit and healthy is to eat a diet of nutritious foods like these.

CHELSEA HOUSE PUBLISHERS

VP, NEW PRODUCT DEVELOPMENT Sally Cheney
DIRECTOR OF PRODUCTION Kim Shinners
CREATIVE MANAGER Takeshi Takahashi
MANUFACTURING MANAGER Diann Grasse

Staff for NUTRITION AND EATING DISORDERS

EXECUTIVE EDITOR Tara Koellhoffer
ASSOCIATE EDITOR Beth Reger
PRODUCTION EDITOR Noelle Nardone
PHOTO EDITOR Sarah Bloom
SERIES & COVER DESIGNER Terry Mallon
LAYOUT 21st Century Publishing and Communications, Inc.

A Haights Cross Communications Company

www.chelseahouse.com

First Printing

9 8 7 6 5 4 3 2 1

Library of Congress Cataloging-in-Publication Data

Smolin, Lori A.
   Nutrition and eating disorders / Lori A. Smolin and Mary B. Grosvenor.
     p. cm. (Eating right)
Includes bibliographical references and index.
   ISBN 0-7910-7851-5 (hard cover)
   1. Nutrition Juvenile literature. 2. Eating disorders Juvenile literature.
I. Grosvenor, Mary B. II. Title. III. Series.
RA784.S5978 2004
616.85'26dc22

                                                    2004010523

All links and Web addresses were checked and verified to be correct at the time of publication. Because of the dynamic nature of the Web, some addresses and links may have changed since publication and may no longer be valid.

Once a reference has been cited, that same number is applied throughout the book to represent the same source.

About the Authors

Lori A. Smolin, Ph.D. Lori Smolin received her B.S. degree from Cornell University, where she studied human nutrition and food science. She received her doctorate from the University of Wisconsin at Madison. Her doctoral research focused on B vitamins, homocysteine accumulation, and genetic defects in homocysteine metabolism. She completed postdoctoral training both at the Harbor–UCLA Medical Center, where she studied human obesity, and at the University of California at San Diego, where she studied genetic defects in amino acid metabolism. She has published in these areas in peer-reviewed journals. She and Mary Grosvenor are coauthors of two well-respected college-level nutrition textbooks and contributing authors to a middle school text. Dr. Smolin is currently at the University of Connecticut, where she teaches both in the Department of Nutritional Sciences and in the Department of Molecular and Cell Biology. Courses she has taught include introductory nutrition, lifecycle nutrition, food preparation, nutritional biochemistry, general biochemistry, and introductory biology.

Mary B. Grosvenor, M.S., R.D. Mary Grosvenor received her B.A. degree in English from Georgetown University and her M.S. in nutrition sciences from the University of California at Davis. She is a registered dietitian with experience in public health, clinical nutrition, and nutrition research. She has published in peer-reviewed journals in the areas of nutrition and cancer and methods of assessing dietary intake. She and Lori Smolin are the coauthors of two well-respected college-level nutrition textbooks and contributing authors to a middle school text. She has

taught introductory nutrition at the community college level and currently lives with her family in a small town in Colorado. She is continuing her teaching and writing career and is still involved in nutrition research via the electronic superhighway.

Contents Overview

Detailed Contents

Preface

Lori A. Smolin, Ph.D.
Mary B. Grosvenor, M.S., R.D.

Fifty years ago we got our nutrition guidance from our mothers and grandmothers—eat your carrots, they are good for your eyes; don't eat too many potatoes, they'll make you fat; be sure to get plenty of roughage so your bowels move. Today, everyone has some advice—take a vitamin supplement to optimize your health; don't eat fish with cabbage because you won't be able to digest them together; you can't stay healthy on a vegetarian diet. Nutrition is one of those topics about which all people seem to think they know something or at least have an opinion. Whether it is the clerk in your local health food store recommending that you buy supplements or the woman behind you in line at the grocery store raving about the latest low-carbohydrate diet—everyone is ready to offer you nutritional advice. How do you know what to believe or, even more important, what to do?

Our purpose in writing these books is to help you answer these questions. As authors, we are students of nutrition. We enjoy studying and learning the hows and whys of each nutrient and other components of our diets. However, despite our enthusiasm about the science of nutrition, we recognize that not everyone loves science or shares this enthusiasm. On the other hand, everyone loves certain foods and wants to stay healthy. In response to this, we have written these books in a way that makes the science you need to understand as palatable as the foods you love. Once you understand the basics, you can apply them to your everyday choices regarding nutrition and health. We have developed one book that includes all the basic nutrition information you need to choose a healthy diet and three others that cover topics that are of special concern to many: weight management, exercise, and eating disorders.

Our goal is not to tell you to stop eating potato chips and candy bars, to give up fast food, or to always eat your vegetables. Instead, it is to provide you with the information you need to make informed choices about your diet. We hope you will recognize that potato chips and candy are not poison, but should only be eaten as occasional treats. We hope you will decide for yourself that fast food is something you can indulge in every now and then, but is not a good choice everyday. We hope you will recognize that although you should eat your vegetables, not everyone always does, so you should do your best to try new vegetables and fruits and eat them as often as possible. These books take the science of nutrition out of the classroom and allow you to apply this information to the choices you make about foods, exercise, dietary supplements, and other lifestyle choices that are important to your health. We hope the knowledge on these pages will help you choose a healthy diet while allowing you to enjoy the diversity of flavors, textures, and tastes that food provides and the meanings that food holds in our society. When you eat a healthy diet, you will feel good in the short term and enjoy health benefits in the long term. We can't personally evaluate your each and every meal, so we hope these books give you the tools to make your own nutritious choices.

This book in the series EATING RIGHT: AN INTRODUCTION TO HUMAN NUTRITION examines why we eat what we do, what we view as an ideal body, and how these and other factors contribute to the development of eating disorders. It examines the many types of eating disorders, including anorexia, bulimia, and binge-eating disorder, and explores the signs and symptoms of each. Despite the fact that the United States today is the fattest society in the history of the world, the media constantly bombard us with body shape ideals that verge on dangerous thinness. This book discusses how an understanding of the cultural and psychological causes of eating disorders can help reduce their incidence.

Lori A. Smolin, Ph.D.
Mary B. Grosvenor, M.S., R.D.

Introduction

Richard J. Deckelbaum, MD, CM, FRCP(C)
Robert R. Williams Professor of Nutrition
Director, Institute of Human Nutrition
College of Physicians and Surgeons of Columbia University

Nutrition is a major factor in optimizing health and performance at every age through the life cycle. While almost everyone recognizes the devastating effects of severe undernutrition, often captured on television during famines in underdeveloped parts of the world, far fewer people recognize the problem of overnutrition that leads to overweight and obesity. Even fewer are aware of the dangers of "hidden malnutrition" associated with inadequate intake of important vitamins and minerals. Unfortunately, there is also an overabundance of inaccurate and misleading nutrition advice being presented through media and books that makes it difficult for teenagers and young adults to decide for themselves what really is "optimal nutrition." This series, EATING RIGHT: AN INTRODUCTION TO HUMAN NUTRITION, provides accurate information to help people of all ages, and particularly young people, to acquire the needed tools and knowledge to integrate good nutrition as part of a healthy lifestyle. Each book in the series will be a comprehensive study in a different area of nutrition and its applications. The series will stress on many levels how healthy food choices affect the ability of people to develop, learn, and be more successful in sports, work, and in passing on good health to their families.

Beginning early in life, proper nutrition has major impacts. In childhood, good nutrition is important not only in allowing normal physical growth, but also in brain development and the ability to acquire new knowledge, both in and out of school. For example, proper dietary intake of iron is critical for preventing anemia, but just as important, it also ensures the ability to learn in the classroom and to be successful in sports or other spheres relating to physical activity. Given the major contribution of sports and exercise in improving health, it is easy to understand that nutrition truly is a partner with physical activity in promoting good health and better life outcomes.

Going into the adolescent years, many teenagers succumb to the dangers of fad diets—for example, undereating or alternatively overeating. Teens may not realize the impact of poor food choices upon their health, and, especially for girls, the risk that improper intake of vitamins and minerals will adversely impact their future families is very much underappreciated. As people mature into adults, nutritional practices have a major role in increasing or preventing the risk of major diseases such as stroke, heart attacks, and even a number of cancers. Thus, proper nutrition is an easy and cost-effective approach to achieving better growth and development, and later in markedly diminishing the chance of contracting many diseases.

Optimizing nutrition not only helps individuals but also has a major impact upon decreasing suffering and economic costs in families, communities, and nations. In the 21st century, individuals and populations will need to focus on at least three key areas. First, in promoting healthy lifestyles, nutrition needs to include a heavy concentration on diet and physical activity. Second, nutrition programs must focus on the realization that it is more important to work toward prevention rather than cure. Many of the early successes in nutrition focus on using nutrition as a treatment. We now know that improvement in nutritional status, which can easily be achieved, will have much more impact on preventing disease before it happens. Third, nutrition fits very well within the life cycle model. We know now that females who are healthy and fit *before* pregnancy are more likely to produce healthy babies and consequently healthy children. Conversely, women who have deficiencies of certain vitamins or unhealthy weights before pregnancy are more likely to have babies and children with significant health problems.

Developing countries now share the worldwide obesity epidemic. This series will help in the understanding that being overweight or obese not only changes physical appearance but also has a number of hidden dangers. For example, overweight and obesity are linked closely to rapid development of cardiovascular disease, type 2 diabetes, respiratory illnesses, and even liver disease and certain lung diseases. This "epidemic" must be fought by combined strategies using diet and physical activity. While many people today are striving to create more healthy lifestyles, they are unsure of how they should proceed. We feel that the books in this series will address these issues and provide the springboards for further thought and consideration about healthy eating.

This book in the series EATING RIGHT: AN INTRODUCTION TO HUMAN NUTRITION presents the facts you need to know to understand and prevent dangerous eating disorders. Along with the other books in the series—*Basic Nutrition, Nutrition and Weight Management,* and *Nutrition for Sports and Exercise*—this book provides the knowledge about nutrition and healthy living that you need to achieve a better outcome for yourself and your family. With the information to be gained through this series, we hope that each reader will be able to enhance his or her commitment to providing a better life for him- or herself and the community.

Richard J. Deckelbaum, MD, CM, FRCP(C)
Robert R. Williams Professor of Nutrition
Director, Institute of Human Nutrition
College of Physicians and Surgeons
of Columbia University

1

The Meaning
of Food

Food provides the energy and raw materials we need to live,
grow, and reproduce. But food does more than meet our physiological
needs. From the time we are born, food is part of our interpersonal
and emotional experience. A loving bond develops between young
children and the caregivers who feed and nurture them. As children
grow and become able to feed themselves, food continues to be
a focus of social interactions and family traditions. Throughout
life, our eating patterns are affected by the society in which we
live. What we have available and what we view as acceptable, both
personally and culturally, affect which foods we choose to eat.
In addition, our individual psychological and emotional states
influence what, when, and how much we eat.

Sometimes it is difficult to separate food's physiological function
from its psychological effects. When food takes on too much importance for reasons other than nutrition, eating behavior may become
abnormal. In the United States today, approximately 3 out of every
100 people are affected by conditions called **eating disorders**. Most

of these people are girls and women in their teens and early twenties. The causes of these disorders are complex and multifaceted, but the emotional and sociocultural meaning that we place on food certainly plays a role.

FOOD AND ITS EMOTIONAL SIGNIFICANCE

From birth, food is linked to affection. As infants suckling while cradled in our mothers' arms, we experienced both physical and emotional satisfaction. This was a time when we were comforted by physical contact and the assurance that we were loved and all our basic needs were being met (Figure 1.1). During childhood, the association between food, affection, and comfort continues to be reinforced. For example, when a child is sick, "comfort food" such as hot tea and chicken soup help him or her feel better. Many of the

---

FACT BOX 1.1

For Love or Chocolate

Few foods are as universally desired as chocolate. It is offered as a reward or treat. It is eaten for comfort and loved for its smooth sweet taste and sensual appeal. When it was first introduced to Europe in the 15th century, it was the food of royalty. Through the centuries, it has been hailed as everything from an antidepressant to an aphrodisiac. What makes it so irresistible?

It turns out that the hold chocolate has on us comes not only from our mouths, but from our heads. Eating chocolate leads the brain to produce natural opiates, which dull pain and increase feelings of well-being.[a] Chocolate also contains a compound called anandamide, which gives us a feeling of well-being, and another chemical called phenylethylamine, which makes blood pressure and blood sugar levels rise, increasing our sensations of alertness and contentment. Chocolate also has caffeine and caffeine-related compounds that make it act as a stimulant. So, there seems to be a physiological as well as a sensual basis for the "chocoholic" in most of us. No wonder Americans buy $5 billion worth of it every year.

[a] Kuwana, E. "Discovering the sweet mysteries of chocolate." Available online at *http://faculty.washington.edu/chudler/choco.html.*

Figure 1.1 Food takes on an emotional meaning beginning with our first meals, which are usually eaten while cradled in our parents' arms.

"comfort foods" we enjoy as adults gained their significance in our childhood. Throughout life, providing food is considered an expression of love and friendship. People serve lemonade or coffee when friends drop by. Our grandparents offer cookies and other treats when we visit. Conversely, refusing food can be interpreted as a personal rejection to the individual who offers it.

We also use food to express or moderate our moods and emotional states. For example, sometimes when people are sad, they bury their sorrows in a chocolate bar or a bowl of ice cream. Some people choose specific foods because they link these foods with comfort, love, and security. Some foods are associated not only with love but also with sexuality. For example, chocolate is a sensual treat that is a traditional Valentine's Day gift.

Food triggers our memories and the emotions that go along with them. Eating the same food today can remind you of an experience or a time earlier in your life. For example, eating a food your mother often served may give you the sense of comfort and security you felt at home as a child. A particular meal you shared with a loved one on a special occasion may bring back the intense emotions you felt at that earlier time. In addition to these positive memories and associations, a bad experience with food may lead you to develop negative associations with certain foods. For instance, if you once became ill after eating a food, you may avoid that food for the rest of your life.

FOOD DEFINES WHO YOU ARE

Food is a part of your personal, socioeconomic, cultural, and religious identity. Sometimes, these identity messages are based on stereotypes. For example, the upper class is associated with meals that are presented on fine china and served with a degree of ceremony. We imagine sophisticated people eating rare, expensive foods such as caviar in an elegant setting. In contrast, we associate the lower class with frozen dinners eaten on trays in front of the television. We assume that vegetarians are concerned about ecology and the environment and that men who eat thick, rare steaks are macho. In fact, we sometimes choose certain foods on purpose to convey a particular image.

Food can also define whether you are good or bad because it is used as a reward or a punishment. A good child is given a cookie, whereas a bad one is sent to bed without dinner. For some of us, this association continues into adulthood because we consider ourselves good when we eat healthy foods and bad when we order a decadent dessert. We reward life's accomplishments with food. A professional success or a new job may be celebrated with a special dinner.

Food can also reflect power relations within a family or culture. Within most cultures, powerful individuals eat well. The head of the family (usually the father) gets the first choice of foods. In some cultures, this tradition is even more extreme. The men get their fill before the women are even allowed to eat at all.

Food is an integral part of our ethnic and religious identity. Individuals from Asian cultures eat rice at every meal and Italians grow up on pasta. Indian cuisine is recognized by curries and Mexican food by refried beans and tortillas. Food patterns and ceremonies are among the most ingrained of all cultural traditions. Almost every religion has dietary rules or restrictions. Seventh-Day Adventists are vegetarians, Jews and Muslims do not eat pork, and Sikhs and Hindus do not eat beef. Devout Jews follow kosher dietary laws. Catholics do not eat meat on Fridays during the season of Lent. Many religions have special foods that are eaten to commemorate religious events or holidays. Muslims do not eat before sundown during the month of Ramadan to recognize the first revelation of the Qur'an (Koran). Jews eat the unleavened bread matzo during Passover to remember their ancestors' flight from slavery in Egypt, which was too hasty to give them time to wait for bread to rise. Christians eat bread and drink wine during church services to commemorate Jesus's Last Supper before his crucifixion.

FOOD AND SOCIAL INTERACTION

Food is a focus of social interaction. At special events, it is symbolic and commemorative. We celebrate marriages and anniversaries with food, and even mourn our dead with feasts. Specific foods define certain holidays, both religious and nonreligious. What would a birthday be without a cake? We eat turkey on Thanksgiving to remember a meal the Pilgrims shared with Native Americans. Each of us associates holidays such as Christmas, Easter, Passover, New Year's, and Kwanzaa with specific foods that are traditional within our families and culture.

Food is also the centerpiece of our everyday social interactions. We get together with friends for meals. The dinner table is often the center for communication within the family—a place where the experiences of the day are shared. Summer outings often center around a picnic or barbecue. This eating is not just for sustenance but is social as well.

WHY DO WE CHOOSE CERTAIN FOODS?

There are lots of reasons we choose to eat the foods we do. Sometimes, it is simply because a particular food is put in front of us, but it also depends on which foods suit our personal or cultural preferences, which foods meet with social acceptance, which foods we are exposed to, and perhaps what we think is a healthy choice.

What Is Available

Availability is a major factor in food choice. The foods available to a person or a population are affected by geography, socioeconomic factors, and health status. In underdeveloped areas, food choices are limited to what is produced locally. In more developed locations, a greater variety is available due to the ability to store, transport, and process food that is grown and produced at distant locations. Even when foods are available in stores, they are not necessarily available to everyone in the population. Socioeconomic factors such as income, education, and the availability of cooking facilities and transportation affect the types of foods different people can choose. People with low incomes must limit the amount of money they spend on food; choice is often based on what is on sale. A lack of knowledge of how to prepare foods can also limit what food choices are available. People who do not have a stove cannot cook foods at home, so they are restricted to eating precooked or cold meals. A college student who

---

FACT BOX 1.2

Eating Out

The modern American lifestyle, with its working parents, single-parent households, and endless after-school events, leaves little time for home-cooked meals. As a result, Americans have come to rely on restaurants and frozen dinners to get them through the week. Americans eat 64 restaurant meals per person every year and 70 take-out meals. When we do eat at home, it is often a frozen meal. In 1994, the American average was about 60 frozen meals per year; this had increased to 74 per year in 2001.

Figure 1.2 Food choices can be limited by what is available. In developing nations, people often have access only to foods grown locally because of inadequate transportation and storage options. Many people in developing nations buy all their food at local outdoor markets like this one.

does not have a refrigerator cannot store perishable foods. Someone without a car can purchase only what he or she can carry home on foot or while riding on a bus or subway (Figure 1.2).

Availability can be affected by lifestyle. Busy modern lives often leave little time to buy food and prepare meals. This is a particular problem in single-parent families or in families in which both parents work. As a result, prepared foods, fast food, and restaurant meals have become a larger and larger part of our dietary pattern.

Health status can also affect the availability of food. People with food allergies, digestive disorders, and dental problems have limited choices in the foods they can eat. People who require special diets for disease conditions can only safely choose foods that meet their dietary prescriptions.

What You Prefer

Availability affects what foods we have to choose from, but individual tastes and cultural, religious, and personal beliefs determine what we eat. We all have our own preferences for taste, smell, appearance, and texture that affect which foods we choose and which we reject. Personal beliefs also influence food choices; a vegetarian will not choose a meal that includes animal products and an environmentalist may not choose a food packaged in a nonrecyclable container.

Creatures of Habit

Your habits are also important factors in determining which foods you choose. The foods and meal patterns you are exposed to as a child influence which foods you buy and cook as an adult. For example, you most likely eat three meals a day and have specific types of foods at these three meals. For most of us, breakfast might include cereal, toast, or eggs, while lunch is made up of soup or sandwiches. Would it seem strange to you to have a peanut butter sandwich for breakfast or a bowl of cereal for dinner? People's eating patterns develop based on what foods they eat during childhood.

What Society Teaches Us

As children, we learn which foods are appropriate to consume under particular social circumstances. As we grow, peer pressure influences our food choices. A child may decide to try a new food because a friend eats it. A teen may change his or her diet to fit in with peers. The amount of food we eat is also affected by social settings. In some cases, we eat more because we are with friends in a social setting. In other cases, we may eat less or choose different foods from what we normally would in order to impress a dining companion. We also might eat foods we typically avoid out of politeness to a host.

What Advertisers Sell Us

The products we see advertised on television and in magazines can influence the foods we choose. Often, the sales of food products are proportional to the money companies spend advertising them. Unfortunately, many of the products that are the focus of advertising campaigns are high in fat or sugar. A review of commercials during children's television shows found that most were for foods high in sugar, fat, and salt.[1]

What We Think Is Good for Us

Our ideas about what makes up a healthy diet affect our food choices. We may choose specific types of foods to try to lose weight. We may limit red meat intake to reduce our risk of heart disease, or purchase organically produced foods because we believe that pesticide exposure is harmful. Health concerns also sell products. Foods marketed to reduce the risk of cancer, lower cholesterol, or improve bone health sell well. For example, a campaign advertising

---

FACT BOX 1.3

Fly Soup

How would you feel if you found a fly in your soup? Most of us would not be too happy; in our culture, we think of insects as contaminants, not food. This is not the case in many places around the world, however. Some societies use insects as a major source of protein. Grasshoppers are eaten in Africa and are becoming popular in South Korea. Termites, which contain more protein per ounce than beef, are a common protein source in parts of Africa and Australia. Caterpillars and other insect larvae are also popular in parts of the world. In Mexico, caterpillars of the Giant Skipper butterfly are a delicacy, and in Africa, the larva of the Goliath beetle is collected from among the roots of the banana tree. Despite our aversion to eating insects, survival manuals point out that insects are a perfect choice when other food sources are not available. In 1995, when American fighter pilot Captain Scott O'Grady was shot down while flying over Bosnia, he survived in the forests by eating ants. For those of you who find this unappealing, consider the fact that a favorite sweetener—honey—is regurgitated by insects in its production.

Source: "Insects as Human Food." Available online at *http://www.si.edu/resource/faq/nmnh/buginfo/inasfood.htm.*

the cholesterol-lowering properties of oats increased the sale of breakfast cereals by $1.5 billion in just two years.

CONNECTIONS

We eat food to meet our physiological needs, but food is much more. Food is also psychologically nurturing. It is part of our personal, social, cultural, and religious identity. It is an essential component of our social interactions. There are many reasons we choose to eat specific foods. Often, it is because certain foods are more available to us in light of geographic or economic factors. What is available, however, also depends on living conditions, lifestyle, and health status. The foods we choose are influenced by our personal preferences for taste, smell, texture, and appearance. We may also have preferences based on our culture and personal convictions. Habits, social factors, exposure to advertising, and our beliefs about nutrition and health also affect food choice.

2

Normal and Abnormal Eating

Food does more than nourish us. As discussed in Chapter 1, it has meaning at the personal, social, cultural, and emotional levels. If our feelings about food come into conflict at any of these levels, it is likely to affect our relationship with food. In such cases, food and eating may take on more significance than is healthy.

WHAT IS NORMAL EATING?

How do you know if you are eating normally? On some days, you may eat twice as much as you do on other days. One day, you may go out for lunch and stuff yourself, and on the next, you may just have a salad for lunch. Some days, you may consume only snack foods because you don't have time to prepare healthy meals, while on other days, you can relax and prepare three balanced meals. Some days, you seem to be hungry all the time, and on others, you seem to have no appetite. All this is normal.

Normal eating patterns are flexible; sometimes people overeat, and sometimes they undereat. What and how much people eat varies in response to emotions, time limitations, hunger, and the proximity of food. Normal eating may sometimes involve constraint in order to choose foods to maintain weight and meet recommendations for a healthy diet. But generally, people eat when they are hungry, choose foods they enjoy, and stop eating when they are satisfied.

WHY DO WE EAT?

In addition to the many meanings food has in our lives, we have a basic biological need to eat. We need food to fuel our bodies and provide it with the essential nutrients that support life. The decision to put food in your mouth at a particular time is the result of the interplay between the biological need for food, the sensory pleasure it provides, and the emotional and sociocultural meanings it holds. This is illustrated by the fact that food consumption is stimulated by both **hunger** and **appetite**. Hunger is the physiological drive to eat food. Appetite is the drive to eat specific foods, which is not necessarily related to hunger. So, we tend to eat lunch around noon both because it has been hours since we had breakfast and our bodies need more food and because social convention dictates that lunch be eaten at or around 12:00 P.M. After we eat, we experience **satiety**, the feeling of fullness and satisfaction that follows food intake and signals us to stop eating. The signals that tell us to eat or to stop eating can be external, coming from the sensory and sociocultural signals all around us, or they can be internal, originating from the gastrointestinal (GI) tract, circulating nutrients, or from higher centers in the brain.

External Factors That Affect Eating Behavior

Some of the same external factors that affect which foods we choose also stimulate or suppress eating behavior in general. These include the sight, taste, and smell of food; the time of day; social conventions; the appeal of the foods available; and cultural or religious rituals. For example, even if you have eaten a meal recently and are not hungry, you may snack on cookies or cinnamon rolls while walking through the mall because the smell entices you to buy them. Likewise, external factors such as religious dietary laws, negative experiences associated with certain foods, or an uncomfortable social setting can encourage you to stop eating. Psychological factors can also affect appetite and eating behavior. Appetite is often closely connected to emotions. The effect that emotions have on appetite depends on the individual. Some people eat for comfort and to relieve stress. Others may lose their appetite when they feel these same emotions.

Internal Factors That Affect Eating Behavior

In addition to external signals, there are signals that come from inside our bodies that stimulate hunger and let us know when we are full. The simplest type of signal about food intake comes from local nerves in the walls of the stomach and small intestine that sense the volume or pressure of food and send a message to the brain to either start or stop food intake. The presence of glucose, fat, and amino

---

FACT BOX 2.1

Are We Conditioned Like Pavlov's Dogs?

Are you hungry at meal times, or does the time of day when a meal is expected make you feel hungry? Long-term associations between food and circumstance, such as the time of day or a particular place, can condition you to expect food and feel hungry when that situation occurs. This desire to eat is due to a conditioned response. It is the same thing that caused Pavlov's dogs to salivate at the sound of a bell. Ivan Pavlov was a Russian scientist who lived a hundred years ago. In 1904, he was awarded the Nobel Prize in Physiology or Medicine for his studies on digestion. While doing experiments on digestion, he noticed that after his experimental dogs got used to a specific feeding routine, they began to salivate just in response to some of the pre-feeding activities. In order to verify this observation, he began to feed his dogs in association with the ringing of a bell. After a time, the dogs began to salivate profusely whenever they heard the ringing bell, even if they could not see or smell any food. Does your mouth water when the clock strikes twelve?

acids in the gastrointestinal tract also sends information directly to the brain and triggers the release of gastrointestinal **hormones** that cause satiety.[2] Absorbed nutrients may also send messages to the brain to influence food intake. Levels of nutrients that circulate through the body, including glucose, amino acids, ketones, and fatty acids, are monitored by the brain and may trigger signals to eat or not to eat.[3] Nutrients that are taken up by the brain may affect **neurotransmitter** concentrations, which then influence the amount and type of nutrients we take in. For example, some studies suggest that when a neurotransmitter called serotonin is low, we crave carbohydrates, but when it is high, we prefer protein. The liver may also be involved in signaling hunger and satiety. Water-soluble nutrients are sent directly to the liver after they are absorbed. Changes in liver metabolism—in particular, the amount of **adenosine triphosphate** (**ATP**)—are believed to modulate food intake. The pancreas is also involved in food intake regulation because it releases insulin, which may affect hunger and satiety by lowering the levels of circulating nutrients. Insulin may also be involved in the long-term regulation of body fat.

Hormones released before and after eating also help regulate when we eat meals and how much we eat. The hormone ghrelin, produced by the stomach, is believed to stimulate our desire to eat meals at the usual times.[4] For example, we typically feel hungry around lunchtime regardless of when we ate and how much food we had for breakfast. Peptide PYY is a hormone that may help us stop eating because it causes a reduction in appetite and food intake. The gastrointestinal tract releases peptide PYY after a meal and the amount released is related to the calorie content of the meal.[5]

WHAT IS ABNORMAL EATING?

Food has many meanings and eating behavior is controlled by many factors. When someone places too much significance on food, eating, and body size and shape, his or her eating patterns may become abnormal. When this happens, the emotional aspects of food and eating can overpower the role of food as nutrition and an eating disorder may develop (Figure 2.1).

Figure 2.1 Abnormal eating may occur when the emotional aspects of food become more important to a person than food's physiological role. This is one of the most obvious characteristics of someone with an eating disorder.

What Are Eating Disorders?

Eating disorders are a group of conditions characterized by a pathological concern with body weight and shape. Eating disorders involve a persistent disturbance in eating behavior or other behaviors intended to control weight. These behaviors affect physical health and psychosocial functioning. They are not due to any other psychiatric or mental condition. However, the term *eating disorder* is something of a misnomer because it implies that the primary problem is abnormal eating behavior. In fact, eating disorders are mainly psychological illnesses that involve nutrition-related behaviors and nutritional and physiological complications. According to mental health guidelines, there are three categories of eating disorders: **anorexia nervosa**, **bulimia nervosa**, and **eating disorders not otherwise specified** (**EDNOS**), which include **binge-eating disorder** (Table 2.1).

Anorexia Nervosa

Anorexia is characterized by extreme weight loss due to rigid dieting or excessive exercise stemming from a fear of being fat. Individuals with anorexia spend a great deal of time thinking about food but eat such small amounts that they may literally starve themselves to death. They have an abnormal perception of their bodies—they see themselves as overweight even when they are dangerously thin.

Bulimia Nervosa

Individuals with bulimia, like those with anorexia, are afraid of weight gain and feel intensely dissatisfied with their bodies. People with the disorder consume large amounts of food over a short period of time in food **binges**, then use behaviors such as vomiting or the taking of laxatives to **purge** the body of the excess calories they have eaten, thus preventing weight gain. People who have bulimia are typically of normal body weight.

Binge-Eating Disorder

Binge-eating disorder is characterized by food binges in which a person eats an excessive amount of food within a discrete

Table 2.1 Characteristics of Different Eating Disorders

	Anorexia	Bulimia	Binge-Eating Disorder
Body weight	Below normal	Normal	Above normal
Binge eating	Possibly	Yes	Yes
Purging	Possibly	Yes	No
Restricts food intake	Yes	Yes	Yes
Body image	Dissatisfaction with body and distorted image of body size	Dissatisfaction with body and distorted image of body size	Dissatisfaction with body
Fear of being fat	Yes	Yes	Not excessive
Self-esteem	Low	Low	Low

period of time. Unlike the bulimia sufferer, however, a person with binge-eating disorder does not use purging behaviors. These people are typically overweight and are very concerned about their appearance.

CONNECTIONS

Normal eating patterns are varied and flexible. Sometimes we exercise restraint and sometimes we choose to overeat, but, in general, we eat when we are hungry or when our appetite is stimulated by outside factors. We choose foods we enjoy, and we usually stop eating when we feel full. Eating disorders develop when people place excessive importance on food, eating behavior, and body

FACT BOX 2.2

The Myths and Realities of Eating Disorders

MYTHS	REALITIES
Only girls get eating disorders.	Although most people with eating disorders are female, the disorders also occur in males.
You can tell that someone has an eating disorder by how he or she looks.	Not all people with eating disorders are extremely thin. Even someone of normal weight could have an eating disorder.
Eating disorders are a nutritional problem.	Although people with eating disorders focus on food and eating, this is only a symptom of underlying psychological problems.
People with bulimia always use vomiting as a way to rid their bodies of excess calories.	Not all bulimics vomit to eliminate excess calories. Some use laxatives, diuretics, exercise, or fasting.
People with anorexia do not binge or purge.	Some people with anorexia do binge and purge occasionally.
You cannot die from bulimia.	Bulimia can be life-threatening, especially in people who use laxatives and exercise excessively.
People cannot have more than one eating disorder at a time.	Many people have more than one eating disorder.

size and shape. The three main types of eating disorders are anorexia nervosa, which is characterized by self-starvation; bulimia nervosa, which involves binging and purging behavior; and binge-eating disorder, which is characterized by binging without purging.

3

How Food Nourishes You

Food nourishes us—both emotionally and physically. People with eating disorders have poor diets because they allow the psychological aspects of food to become more important than the physiological factors. To understand the physiological and nutritional problems caused by disordered eating, and the importance of diet and nutrition in treatment, it is essential to have a basic understanding of **nutrition**, the science that studies all of the interactions that occur between people and food. Nutrition involves understanding which **nutrients** we need, where to find them in food, how they are used by our bodies, and the impact they have on our health. It also has to consider other factors, such as society and culture, economics and technology, and psychology and emotions, which all play a role in choosing the foods we eat.

WE GET NUTRIENTS FROM FOOD

We don't eat individual nutrients, we eat foods. When we choose the right combination of foods, our diet provides all the nutrients we need to stay healthy. If we choose a poor combination of foods, we may be missing out on some **essential nutrients**. Even with a knowledge of nutrition, choosing a diet that provides all the essential nutrients can be challenging because, as illustrated in the previous chapters, we eat for many reasons other than to obtain nutrients.

The Nutrients in Food

There are more than 40 nutrients that are essential to human life. We need to consume these nutrients in our diets because they cannot be made in our bodies or cannot be made in large enough amounts to optimize health. Different foods contain different nutrients in varying amounts and combinations. For example, beef, chicken, and fish provide protein, vitamin B_6, and iron; bread, rice, and pasta provide carbohydrates, folic acid, and niacin; fruits and vegetables provide carbohydrates, fiber, vitamin A, and vitamin C; and vegetable oils provide fat and vitamin E. In addition to the nutrients found naturally in foods, many foods have nutrients added to them to replace losses that occur during cooking and processing, or to supplement the diet. Dietary supplements are also a source of nutrients. Although most people can meet their nutrient needs without them, supplements can be useful for maintaining health and preventing deficiencies.

What Do Nutrients Do?

Nutrients perform three basic functions in the body. Some nutrients provide energy, some provide structure, and others help regulate the processes that keep us alive. Each nutrient performs one or more of these functions, and all nutrients together are needed for growth, to maintain and repair the body, and to allow us to reproduce.

Energy

Food provides the body with the energy or fuel it needs to stay alive, to move, and to grow. This energy keeps your heart pumping, your lungs inhaling, and your body warm. It is also used to keep your stomach churning and your muscles working. Carbohydrates, lipids, and proteins are the only nutrients that provide energy to the body;

they are referred to as the energy-yielding nutrients. The energy used by the body is measured in **Calories** or **kilocalories** (abbreviated as "kcalories" or "kcals") or in **kilojoules** (abbreviated as "kjoules" or "kJs"). When spelled with a lowercase "c," the term *calorie* is technically 1/1,000 of a kilocalorie. Each gram of carbohydrate we eat provides the body with 4 Calories. A gram of protein also provides 4 Calories; a gram of fat provides 9 Calories, more than twice the calories of carbohydrates or protein. For this reason, foods that are high in fat are also high in calories. Alcohol can also provide energy in the diet—7 Calories per gram—but it is not considered a nutrient because the body does not need it.

If you eat more calories than you use, your body will store the extra energy, mostly as body fat. When you take in the same number of calories as you use, your body weight remains the same. If you eat fewer calories than you use, your body will use its stored energy to fuel itself and you will lose weight.

Structure

Nutrients help form body structures. For example, the minerals calcium and phosphorus make our bones and teeth hard. Protein forms the structure of our muscles, and lipids are the major component of our body fat. Water is a structural nutrient because it plumps up our cells, giving them shape.

Regulation

Nutrients are also important regulators of body functions. All of the processes that occur in our bodies, from the breakdown of carbohydrates and fat to provide energy, to the building of bone and muscle to form body structures, must be regulated for the body to function normally. For instance, the chemical reactions that maintain body temperature at 98.6°F (37°C) must be regulated or body temperature will rise above or fall below the healthy range. Many different nutrients are important in regulating **homeostasis** in the body. Carbohydrates help to label proteins that must be removed from the blood. Water helps to regulate body temperature. Lipids are needed to make regulatory molecules called hormones, and certain protein molecules, vitamins, and minerals help control the rate of chemical reactions within the body.

Getting Nutrients to Your Cells

The food we eat must be digested and the nutrients must be absorbed so they can function in the body. **Digestion** breaks food into small molecules and **absorption** brings these substances into the body, where they are transported to the cells that need them.

The digestive system is responsible for breaking down and absorbing food (Figure 3.1). The main part of this system is the gastrointestinal tract, also called the GI tract. This hollow tube starts at the mouth. From there, food passes down the esophagus into the stomach and then on to the small intestine. Rhythmic contractions of the smooth muscles that line the GI tract help mix food and push it along. Substances such as **mucus** and **enzymes** are secreted into the gastrointestinal tract to help with the movement and digestion of food. The digestive system also secretes hormones into the blood that help regulate GI activity. Most of the digestion and absorption of nutrients takes place in the small intestine. The blood carries absorbed nutrients to the cells where they are needed. Anything that is not absorbed passes into the large intestine, or colon. Here, some nutrients can be absorbed and wastes are prepared for elimination from the body.

How Your Body Uses Nutrients

Once they get inside body cells, carbohydrates, lipids, and proteins are involved in chemical reactions that allow them to be used for energy or to build other substances that the human body needs. The sum of these chemical reactions that occur inside body cells is called **metabolism**. The chemical reactions of metabolism can synthesize the molecules needed to form body structures such as muscles, nerves, and bones. The reactions of metabolism also break down carbohydrates, lipids, and proteins to yield energy in the form of ATP (adenosine triphosphate). ATP is a molecule that is used by cells as an energy source to do work, such as pumping blood, contracting muscles, or creating new body tissues.

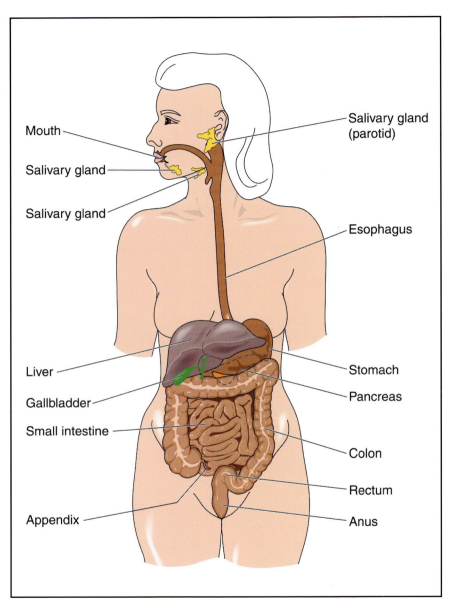

Figure 3.1 The digestive system consists of the gastrointestinal (GI) tract and the accessory organs that aid digestion. This series of interrelated organs provides the body with its nutritional needs. When someone has an eating disorder, he or she risks doing severe damage to the digestive system.

THE SIX CLASSES OF NUTRIENTS

The nutrients we need come from six different classes: carbohydrates, lipids, protein, water, vitamins, and minerals. Each class, with the exception of water, contains a variety of different molecules that the body uses in different ways. Some classes of nutrients are needed in relatively large amounts, whereas others meet needs when only tiny

FACT BOX 3.1

Bacteria in Your Intestine

Did you know that your large intestine is home to several hundred species of bacteria? You provide them with a nice warm home with lots of food and they do you some favors in return—if they are the right kind. These bacteria improve the digestion and absorption of essential nutrients; synthesize some vitamins; and break down harmful substances, such as ammonia, thus reducing levels in the blood. They protect the intestines against disease, help cells in the large intestine grow properly, and keep food moving quickly through the digestive tract. A healthy population of intestinal bacteria may also help prevent constipation, flatulence, and too much stomach acid. However, if the wrong bacteria take over, you could get diarrhea, infections, and perhaps an increased risk of cancer.

How can you make sure the right bacteria are growing in your gut? One way is to eat the bacteria. This is referred to as probiotic therapy. Live bacteria are found in foods such as yogurt and acidophilus milk and can be bought in pill or liquid forms. One problem with probiotic therapy is that the bacteria get washed out of the colon if you stop eating them. A second way to modify the bacteria in your gut is to eat foods or other substances that encourage the growth of particular types of bacteria. Substances that pass undigested into the large intestine and serve as food for these bacteria are called prebiotics. Prebiotics are sold as dietary supplements—but don't run to the store just yet. For most of us, eating a nutritious diet supports a healthy population of intestinal bacteria. Our understanding of how probiotics and prebiotics can be used to treat disease and promote health is still in its early stages.

amounts are consumed. Carbohydrates, lipids, protein, and water are often referred to as **macronutrients** because they are required in the diet in relatively large amounts. Vitamins and minerals are referred to as **micronutrients** because they are needed in only small amounts in the diet.

Carbohydrates

Carbohydrates include sugars, **starches**, and **fibers**. Sugars are the simplest form of carbohydrate. They taste sweet and are found in fruit, milk, and added sugars such as honey and table sugar. Starches are made of multiple sugar units linked together. They do not taste sweet and are found in cereals, grains, and starchy vegetables like potatoes. Starches and sugars are good sources of energy in the diet. Most fibers are also carbohydrates. Good sources of fiber include whole grains, legumes, fruits, and vegetables. Fiber provides little energy to the body because it cannot be digested or absorbed. It is, however, important for the health of the digestive tract.

Lipids

Lipids are commonly called fats. Fat is a concentrated source of energy in our diet and in our bodies. Most fat is in the form of **triglycerides**. Each triglyceride contains three **fatty acids**. Fatty acids are basically chains of carbon atoms. Depending on how these carbons are linked together, fats are classified as either saturated or unsaturated. **Saturated fats** are found mostly in animal products such as meat, milk, and butter. **Unsaturated fats** come from vegetable oils. Small amounts of certain unsaturated fatty acids are essential in the diet. **Cholesterol** is another type of fat found in animal foods. Diets high in saturated fat and cholesterol may increase the risk of heart disease.

Protein

Protein is needed for growth, maintenance and repair of body structures, and for the synthesis of regulatory molecules. It can also be broken down to produce energy. Protein is made of folded chains of **amino acids**. The right amounts and types of amino acids must be consumed in the diet to meet the body's protein needs. Animal foods such as meat, poultry, fish, eggs, and dairy products generally supply a combination of amino acids that meets human needs better than plant proteins do. However, a vegetarian diet that includes only plant foods such as grains, nuts, seeds, vegetables, and legumes can also meet protein needs.

Water

Water is an essential nutrient that makes up about 60% of the adult human body. It provides no energy, but the body needs it to transport nutrients, oxygen, waste products, and other important substances. It also is needed for many chemical reactions, for body structure and protection, and to regulate body temperature. Water is found in beverages as well as solid foods.

Vitamins

Vitamins are small **organic molecules** needed to regulate metabolic processes. They are found in almost all the foods we eat but no one food is a good source of all of them. Some vitamins dissolve in water and others in fat, a property that affects how they are absorbed into and transported throughout the body. Vitamins do not provide energy but many are needed to regulate the chemical reactions that produce usable energy in the body. Some vitamins are **antioxidants**, which protect the body from reactive oxygen compounds like **free radicals**. Others have roles in tissue growth and development, bone health, and blood clotting.

Minerals

Minerals are single **elements**. Some are needed in the diet in significant amounts, whereas the requirements for others are extremely small. Like vitamins, minerals provide no energy but perform a number of diverse functions. Some are needed to regulate chemical reactions, some participate in processes that protect cells from oxidative reactions, and others play roles in bone formation and maintenance, oxygen transport, or immune function.

HOW MUCH OF EACH NUTRIENT DO YOU NEED?

To stay healthy, you need to consume adequate amounts of energy and of each of the essential nutrients in your diet. The amount of each nutrient that you need depends on your age, size, sex, genetic makeup, lifestyle, and health status. General guidelines for the amounts of nutrients people need are made by the **Dietary Reference Intakes** (**DRIs**). The DRIs were developed by teams of American and Canadian scientists who reviewed all the current research and came up with recommendations for the amounts of energy, nutrients, and other substances that will best meet needs and maintain health.[6] These recommendations are general guidelines for the amounts of nutrients that should be consumed on an average daily basis in order to promote health, prevent deficiencies, and reduce the incidence of chronic disease. The exact amount of any nutrient that an individual needs depends on his or her individual circumstances.

The DRIs

The DRIs include recommendations for amounts of energy, nutrients, and other food components for different groups of people, based on age, gender, and, where appropriate, pregnancy and lactation.

The recommendations for energy intakes are expressed as **Estimated Energy Requirements** (**EERs**). These can be used to estimate an individual's energy needs (see Appendix A). The recommendations for nutrient intakes include four different types of values. The **Estimated Average Requirement** (**EAR**) is the amount of a nutrient that is believed to meet the average needs of the population. It is not used to assess individual intake but rather is designed for planning and evaluating how adequate the nutrient intake of population groups is. The **Recommended Dietary Allowances** (**RDAs**) and **Adequate Intakes** (**AIs**) are values calculated to meet the needs of nearly all healthy people in each gender and life-stage group. These can be used to plan and assess individuals' diets. The fourth set of DRI values is the **Tolerable Upper Intake Levels** (**ULs**). These are the maximum levels of intake that are unlikely to pose a risk of adverse health effects. ULs can be used as a guide to limit intake and evaluate the possibility of overconsumption. When your diet provides the RDA or AI for each nutrient and does not exceed the UL for any, your risk of a nutrient deficiency and toxicity is low.

What Happens if You Get Too Little or Too Much?

Consuming either too much or too little of one or more nutrients or of energy can cause **malnutrition**. Typically, we think of malnutrition as a deficiency of energy or nutrients. This may occur due to an inadequate intake, increased requirements, or an inability to absorb or use nutrients. The effects of malnutrition reflect the function of the nutrient in the body and may appear rapidly or may take months or years to appear. For example, vitamin D is needed for strong bones. If children don't get enough of it, their legs will bow outward because they are too weak to support the body weight. We need vitamin A for healthy eyes; a deficiency can result in blindness. For many nutrient deficiencies, supplying the lacking nutrient can quickly reverse the symptoms.

Overnutrition, an excess of energy or nutrients, is also a form of malnutrition. Too much energy causes obesity. It increases the risk of developing diseases such as diabetes and heart disease. Excesses of vitamins and minerals rarely occur from eating food but are seen when people overuse dietary supplements. For example, taking too much vitamin B_6 can cause nerve damage and excess iron intake can cause liver failure.

TOOLS FOR CHOOSING A HEALTHY DIET

Knowing which nutrients your body needs to stay healthy is the first step in choosing a healthy diet, but knowing how many milligrams of niacin, micrograms of vitamin B_{12}, grams of fiber, and what percentage of calories you need from carbohydrates doesn't help you decide what to pack for lunch. Therefore, a variety of tools has been developed to help consumers plan healthy diets. Three of these are food labels, the Food Guide Pyramid, and the Dietary Guidelines for Americans. Using each of these tools can help people choose diets to meet their needs.

Understanding Food Labels

Food labels are a tool designed to help consumers make healthy food choices. They provide information about which nutrients are in individual foods and show how the foods fit into the recommendations for a healthy diet.

The law requires almost all packaged foods to carry a standard nutrition label. Exceptions are raw fruits, vegetables, fish, meat, and poultry. For these foods, nutritional information is often posted on placards in the grocery store or printed in brochures. Food labels must include both an ingredient list and a "Nutrition Facts" panel.

FACT BOX 3.2

What Can You Believe?

Product labels and literature often make fabulous claims about the nutritional benefits of the products. Can you believe everything you read? How can you tell what is fact and what is fantasy?

Generally, the rule is, if it sounds too good to be true, it probably is. The following tips offer some suggestions for evaluating nutritional claims:

- **Think about it.** Does the information presented make sense? If not, disregard it.

- **Consider the source.** Where did the information come from? If it is based on personal opinions, be aware that one person's perception does not make something true.

- **Ponder the purpose.** Is the information helping to sell a product? Is it making a magazine cover or newspaper headline more appealing? If so, the claims may be exaggerated to help the sale.

- **View it skeptically.** If a statement claims to be based on a scientific study, think about who did the study, what their credentials are, and what relationship they have to the product. Do they benefit from the sale of the product?

- **Evaluate the risks.** Be sure the expected benefit of the product is worth the risk associated with using it.

Ingredient List

The ingredient list includes all of the ingredients used when preparing a food, including food additives, colors, and flavorings. The ingredients are listed in order of their prominence by weight. A label that lists water first indicates that most of the weight of that food is water. You can look at the ingredient list if you are trying to avoid certain foods, such as animal products, or a food to which you have an allergy.

Nutrition Facts

The "Nutrition Facts" portion of a food label (Figure 3.2) lists the serving size of the food followed by the total Calories, Calories from fat, total fat, saturated fat, cholesterol, sodium, total carbohydrate, dietary fiber, sugars, and protein per serving of the food. The amounts of these nutrients are given by weight and as a percent of the Daily Value. **Daily Values** are standards developed for food labels. They help consumers see how a food fits into their overall diet. For example, if a food provides 10% of the Daily Value for fiber, then the food provides 10% of the daily recommendation for fiber in a 2,000-Calorie diet. The amounts of vitamin A, vitamin C, iron, and calcium are also listed as a percent of the Daily Value.

In addition to the required nutrition information, food labels often highlight specific characteristics of a product that might be of interest to the consumer. For example, they might advertise that the food is "low in calories" or "high in fiber." The Food and Drug Administration (FDA) has developed definitions for these nutrient content descriptors. Food labels are also allowed to include specific health claims if they are relevant. These are only permitted on labels if the scientific evidence for the claim is reviewed by the FDA and found to be factual.

The Food Guide Pyramid

The Food Guide Pyramid is a visual tool for planning your diet that divides foods into five food groups based on their nutrient composition (Figure 3.3). Choosing the recommended number of

How to Read a Nutrition Facts Label

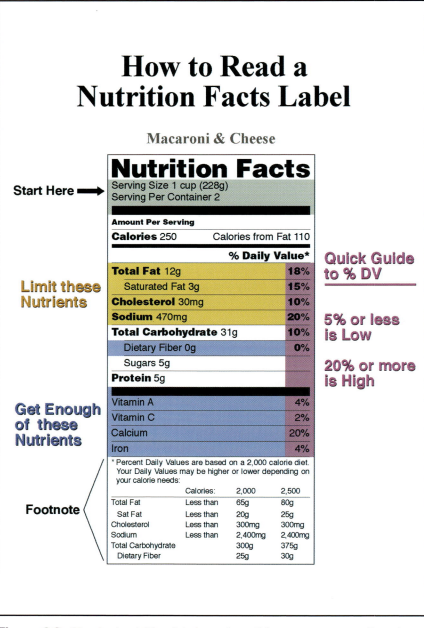

Figure 3.2 Standard nutrition labels such as this one appear on all packaged foods, as required by law. They show how many nutrients a particular food contains.

The Food Guide Pyramid

A Guide to Daily Food Choices

KEY
◻ **Fat** (naturally occurring and added)
■ **Sugars** (added)

These symbols show fat and added sugars in foods.

Fats, Oils, & Sweets
USE SPARINGLY

Milk, Yogurt,
& Cheese
Group
2-3 SERVINGS

Meat, Poultry, Fish,
Dry Beans, Eggs,
& Nuts Group
2-3 SERVINGS

Vegetable
Group
3-5 SERVINGS

Fruit
Group
2-4 SERVINGS

Bread, Cereal,
Rice, & Pasta
Group
**6-11
SERVINGS**

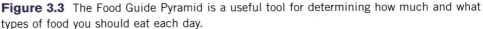

Figure 3.3 The Food Guide Pyramid is a useful tool for determining how much and what types of food you should eat each day.

servings from each group and following the selection tips shown in Table 3.1 will provide a diet that meets nutrient requirements and the recommendations for health promotion and disease prevention. The shape of the Pyramid helps emphasize the recommendations for the amounts of food from each of five food groups. The wide base of the Pyramid is the Bread, Cereal, Rice, & Pasta Group; choosing between 6 and 11 servings of mostly whole grains forms the foundation of a healthy diet. The next level of the Pyramid includes the Vegetable Group, of which 3 to 5 servings per day are recommended,

Table 3.1 Servings and Selections From the Food Guide Pyramid

FOOD GROUP/SERVING SIZE	NUTRIENTS PROVIDED	SELECTION TIPS
Bread, Cereal, Rice, & Pasta **(6 to 11 servings)** 1/2 cup cooked cereal, rice, or pasta 1 ounce dry cereal 1 slice bread 1 tortilla 2 cookies 1/2 medium doughnut	B vitamins Fiber Iron Magnesium Zinc Complex carbohydrates	• Choose whole-grain breads, cereals, and grains such as whole wheat or rye, oatmeal, and brown rice. • Use high-fat, high-sugar baked goods such as cakes, cookies, and pastries in moderation. • Limit fats and sugars added as spreads, sauces, or toppings.
Vegetable **(3 to 5 servings)** 1/2 cup cooked or raw chopped vegetables 1 cup raw leafy vegetables 3/4 cup vegetable juice 10 french fries	Vitamin A Vitamin C Folate Magnesium Iron Fiber	• Eat a variety of vegetables, including dark-green leafy vegetables like spinach and broccoli, deep-yellow vegetables like carrots and sweet potatoes, starchy vegetables such as potatoes and corn, and other vegetables such as green beans and tomatoes. • Cook by steaming or baking. • Avoid frying, and limit high-fat spreads or dressings.
Fruit **(2 to 4 servings)** 1 medium apple, banana, or orange 1/2 cup chopped, cooked, or canned fruit 3/4 cup fruit juice 1/4 cup dried fruit	Vitamin A Vitamin C Potassium Fiber	• Choose fresh fruit, frozen fruit without sugar, dried fruit, or fruit canned in water or juice. • If canned in heavy syrup, rinse fruit with water before eating. • Eat whole fruits more often than juices; they are higher in fiber. • Regularly eat citrus fruits, melons, or berries rich in vitamin C. • Only 100% fruit juice should be counted as fruit.

and the Fruit Group, of which 2 to 4 servings per day are recommended. To meet these recommendations, the "5-a-day" health campaign encourages consumers to include at least 5 fruits and

FOOD GROUP/SERVING SIZE	NUTRIENTS PROVIDED	SELECTION TIPS
Milk, Yogurt, & Cheese (2 to 3 servings) 1 cup milk or yogurt 1-1/2 ounces natural cheese 2 ounces processed cheese 2 cups cottage cheese 1-1/2 cups ice cream 1 cup frozen yogurt	Protein Calcium Riboflavin Vitamin D	• Use low-fat or skim milk for healthy people over 2 years of age. • Choose low-fat and nonfat yogurt, "part skim" and low-fat cheeses, and lower-fat frozen desserts like ice milk and frozen yogurt. • Limit high-fat cheeses and ice cream.
Meat, Poultry, Fish, Dry Beans, Eggs, & Nuts (2 to 3 servings) 2–3 ounces cooked lean meat, fish, or poultry 2–3 eggs 4–6 tablespoons peanut butter 1 to 1-1/2 cups cooked dry beans 2/3 to 1 cup nuts	Protein Niacin Vitamin B_6 Vitamin B_{12} Other B vitamins Iron Zinc	• Select lean meat, poultry without skin, and dry beans often. • Trim fat, and cook by broiling, roasting, grilling, or boiling rather than frying. • Limit egg yolks, which are high in cholesterol, and nuts and seeds, which are high in fat. • Be aware of serving size; 3 ounces of meat is the size of an average hamburger.
Fats, Oils, & Sweets (use sparingly) Butter Mayonnaise Salad dressing Cream cheese Sour cream Jam Jelly	Fat-soluble vitamins	• These are high in energy and low in micronutrients. • Substitute low-fat dressings and spreads.

Human Nutrition Information Service. *The Food Guide Pyramid*. Home and Garden Bulletin No. 252. Hyattsville, MD: U.S. Department of Agriculture, 1992, 1996, revised.

vegetables in their daily diet. The next level, where the decreasing size of the Pyramid boxes reflects the smaller number of recommended servings, comprises the Milk, Yogurt, & Cheese Group and the Meat, Poultry, Fish, Dry Beans, Eggs, & Nuts Group. Two to 3 servings a day are recommended from each of these groups. The narrow tip of the Pyramid consists of a recommendation to use Fats, Oils, & Sweets sparingly in the diet.

The Food Guide Pyramid can be used to plan diets to meet a variety of energy needs. For example, a 45-kilogram (100 lb.) sedentary woman who needs only 1,600 Calories per day could meet her needs by choosing 6 servings of breads and cereals, 3 vegetables, 2 fruits, 2 milk servings, and 2 meat servings. In contrast, a 91-kilogram (200-lb.) teenage boy who needs 2,800 Calories per day could meet his needs by choosing 11 servings of breads and grains, 5 vegetables, 4 fruits, 3 milk servings, and 3 meat servings. The Pyramid is also flexible enough to suit the preferences of people from diverse cultures and lifestyles. For instance, a Mexican American might choose tortillas as a grain, while a Japanese American might prefer rice; a vegetarian may choose beans from the meat and meat substitute group, while someone else might prefer beef.

The Dietary Guidelines

The Dietary Guidelines for Americans is another useful tool that can help you choose a healthy diet. It is a set of recommendations for diet and lifestyle designed to promote health, support active lives, and reduce chronic disease risks. The guidelines are organized into three tiers: the ABCs for Good Health (Figure 3.4).

The first tier, called "Aim for Fitness," includes two guidelines that recommend that we "Aim for a healthy weight" and "Be physically active each day." These guidelines are backed up by specific recommendations for body weight and activity levels.

The "Build a Healthy Base" tier offers four guidelines on choosing a variety of foods and handling these foods safely. It recommends that we let the Food Pyramid guide our food choices; eat a variety of grains, especially whole grains, daily; eat a variety of fruits and vegetables daily; and "Keep food safe to eat."

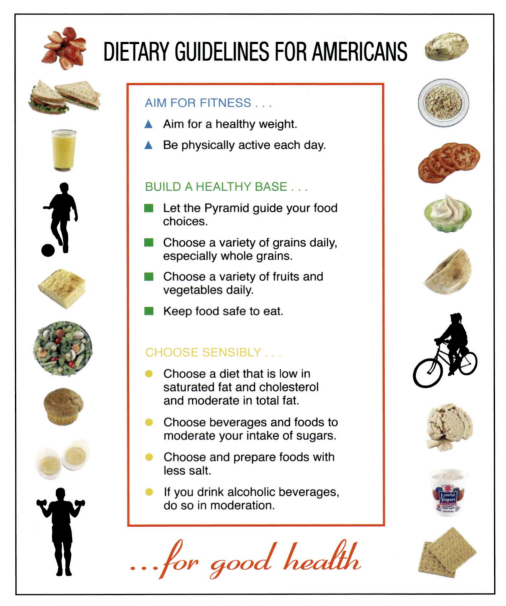

DIETARY GUIDELINES FOR AMERICANS

AIM FOR FITNESS . . .

▲ Aim for a healthy weight.

▲ Be physically active each day.

BUILD A HEALTHY BASE . . .

■ Let the Pyramid guide your food choices.

■ Choose a variety of grains daily, especially whole grains.

■ Choose a variety of fruits and vegetables daily.

■ Keep food safe to eat.

CHOOSE SENSIBLY . . .

● Choose a diet that is low in saturated fat and cholesterol and moderate in total fat.

● Choose beverages and foods to moderate your intake of sugars.

● Choose and prepare foods with less salt.

● If you drink alcoholic beverages, do so in moderation.

. . . for good health

Figure 3.4 The Dietary Guidelines for Americans can help a person choose a healthy and sensible diet. These guidelines suggest that people get enough exercise; choose a variety of different, nutritious foods; and limit their intake of certain food components, such as salt, sugar, and cholesterol.

The last tier, "Choose Sensibly," recommends limiting intakes of certain dietary components. The first guideline, "Choose a diet that is low in saturated fat and cholesterol and moderate in total fat," reflects the understanding that diets low in saturated fat and cholesterol may

---

FACT BOX 3.3

How Healthy Is the American Diet?

A healthy diet should be based on whole grains, vegetables, and fruits, with smaller amounts of dairy products and high-protein foods and limited amounts of fats and sweets. In general, the American diet doesn't meet these recommendations. The Dietary Guidelines and the Food Guide Pyramid recommend that we choose whole rather than refined grains, but the average American eats only one serving of whole grains per day. The Food Guide Pyramid recommends 2–4 servings of fruit, but the average person eats only 1-2/3 each day and 48% of Americans don't have even one piece of fruit daily. We also fall short of the 2–3 servings of dairy products recommended. Americans on average eat only 1-1/2 dairy servings daily and only 12% of teenage girls and 14% of women consume the recommended amounts.[a] In addition to missing out on the benefits of whole grains, fruit, and dairy products, we eat too much added sugar. The average American consumes about 64 pounds of sugar a year, or about 20 teaspoons a day, of added sugar, mostly from soft drinks. Americans drink over 13 billion gallons of soda every year.[b] The typical American diet, along with a lack of physical activity, contributes to the development of chronic diseases, such as diabetes, obesity, heart disease, and cancer, which are the major causes of illness and death in the U.S. population. One estimate suggests that 14% of all premature deaths in the United States can be attributed to diet and a sedentary lifestyle. Recommendations for reducing disease risk focus on increasing activity patterns and choosing a diet that meets recommendations.

a Cleveland, E., J.E. Cook, J.W. Wilson, et al. "Pyramid Servings Data from the 1994 CSFII data." ARS Food Survey Research. Available online at *http://www.barc.usda.gov/bhnrc/foodsurveys/home.html*.

b "Pouring Rights: Marketing Empty Calories." *Public Health Reports 2000*, Vol. 115. New York: Oxford University Press, 2000, pp. 308–319.

reduce the risk of heart disease. The guideline to "Choose beverages and foods to moderate your intake of sugars" is based on the fact that the intake of sugars in the United States has been on the rise and may be increasing the incidence of chronic disease. "Choose and prepare foods with less salt" is based on research that indicates that a diet high in salt increases blood pressure in some individuals. The final guideline emphasizes the dangers of excess alcohol consumption.

CONNECTIONS

Human nutrition is the science that studies the interactions between people and food. Food provides nutrients, which are substances required in the diet for growth, reproduction, and maintenance of the body. There are six classes of nutrients. Carbohydrates include sugars, starches, and fibers. Sugars and starches provide energy at a rate of 4 Calories per gram. Fibers provide little energy because they cannot be digested by human enzymes and, therefore, cannot be absorbed. Lipids are a concentrated source of calories in the diet and in the body, providing 9 Calories per gram. They are also needed to synthesize structural and regulatory molecules. Proteins are made from amino acids. In the body, proteins can provide energy but are more important for their structural and regulatory roles. Water is the most abundant nutrient in the body. Water intake must equal output to maintain balance. Vitamins and minerals are needed in the diet in small amounts. They both have regulatory roles and some minerals also provide structure. Consuming too much or too little energy or nutrients results in malnutrition. The Dietary Reference Intakes (DRIs) recommend amounts of energy and nutrients needed to promote health, prevent deficiencies, and reduce the incidence of chronic disease. The Daily Values on food labels, the Food Guide Pyramid, and the Dietary Guidelines for Americans provide recommendations for choosing foods that will provide these nutrients.

4
Eating Disorders: Who Is Affected and Why?

Eating disorders affect 5–10 million Americans, and thousands of people die each year from their complications.[7] Although some groups are at a greater risk than others, eating disorders occur in people of all ages, races, and socioeconomic backgrounds. We do not know what causes eating disorders, but many factors have been identified that may play a role.

WHO DEVELOPS EATING DISORDERS?

Eating disorders most commonly begin in adolescence, when physical, psychological, and social development is occurring rapidly. Eating disorders are more common in young women than in men. They have typically been associated with Caucasians of higher socioeconomic classes, but they occur in all ethnic and economic groups. Today, eating disorders are as common among Hispanics as they are among Caucasian females, and they occur with greater frequency among Native Americans and lower frequency among African-American and Asian-American females.[8] Eating disorders are more prevalent in groups within the population that are concerned with weight and body image.[9] For example, eating disorders are on the rise among athletes, especially those involved in sports that require the athlete to be thin, such as gymnastics and figure skating, or to fit into a particular weight class, as in wrestling.

Scientists estimate that approximately 1% of female adolescents have anorexia nervosa and 4% of college-age women have bulimia nervosa.[10] In North America, where young women are particularly concerned with body image, being thin is associated with beauty, success, intelligence, and vitality. No American girl wants to be plump. Young women find themselves in a world where they are expected to be independent, have a prestigious job, maintain a successful love relationship, bear and nurture children, manage a household, and stay in fashion. These pressures may make them feel they are unable to control all aspects of their life, so they turn to food intake and body weight as an area in which they can exercise control. These are natural choices, because society tells us that being thin brings success.

Only an estimated 5 to 15% of people with anorexia or bulimia and an estimated 35% of those with binge-eating disorder are male.[11] The gender difference is likely due to both biological and cultural factors, but most research has focused on cultural factors. The increased risk in women has been hypothesized to be related to women's subordinate position in society and their socialization to fit specific gender roles. Compared with men, women are less likely to have access to positions of power, usually earn less money, and experience more sexual abuse and harassment. These factors increase the risks of developing eating disorders. Women are encouraged by society to pursue physical attractiveness, which, in combination with the female beauty ideal of extreme thinness, also increases their risks of developing eating disorders.

Although most eating disorders occur in individuals who are in their teens or early twenties, they also develop in children. As messages about the importance of thinness have become more and more pervasive, eating disorders have begun to appear in children of younger ages. Eating disorders in individuals under the age of 13 are considered childhood-onset eating disorders (see Chapter 9). The causes of these disorders are thought to be the same as the causes among older individuals.

A group that is at high risk for developing eating disorders is athletes who participate in sports that emphasize appearance and a lean body such as ballet and other dance, figure skating, gymnastics, running, swimming, rowing, horse racing, wrestling, ski jumping, and riding. Athletes are under extreme pressure to achieve and maintain a body weight that optimizes their performance. Failure to meet weight goals can have serious consequences such as being cut from the team or restricted from competition. This pressure may lead athletes to follow extreme diets to lose or gain weight at an unhealthy rate. This, combined with the self-motivation and discipline that characterizes successful athletes, makes them vulnerable to eating disorders.

WHAT CAUSES EATING DISORDERS?

We know that eating disorders involve serious disturbances in eating behavior and extreme concern about body size or weight. We also know that eating disorders can be life-threatening if treatment is not provided or is not effective. But we do not completely understand what causes eating disorders. Generally, scientists believe they arise from a complex interaction of genetic, psychological, and sociocultural factors (Figure 4.1).

Genetics and Eating Disorders

Some of the risk of developing anorexia nervosa and bulimia nervosa appears to be inherited. Eating disorders run in families—they are several times more common among the biological relatives of those with anorexia and bulimia than in the general population.[12] Studies done with twins also suggest that genetics plays a role in the development of both anorexia and bulimia—about half the vulnerability of developing an eating disorder is inherited.[12]

Researchers are just beginning to identify **genes** that may be involved in the development of eating disorders. Genes contribute to personality traits and other biological characteristics that are related to eating disorders. For example, inherited abnormalities in the

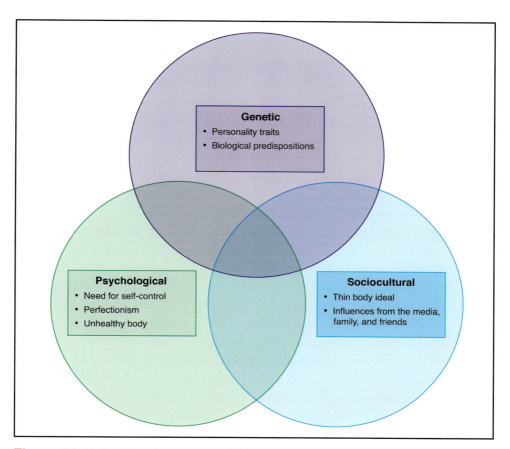

Figure 4.1 Eating disorders are caused by a combination of genetic, psychological, and social factors. All of these aspects must be addressed by medical professionals if treatment is to lead to an effective recovery.

levels of neurotransmitters such as serotonin and their metabolites, and in levels of the hormone leptin, which helps regulate body weight, have been hypothesized to contribute to the behaviors typical of anorexia and bulimia.[13] Binge-eating disorder may be linked to a defect in a gene called the melanocortin-4 receptor gene. The protein made by this gene helps control appetite in the portion of the brain called the hypothalamus, which regulates hunger and satiety. If this gene is abnormal and makes too little protein, the body feels too much hunger. In one study, all carriers of the mutant gene were binge eaters and mutations were found in 5% of obese subjects.[14] Genes like this one contribute to eating disorders, but a single gene is not likely to be the sole cause. Eating disorders are complex diseases that result from the interaction of multiple genes with the environment. Each gene may have a small effect, but, when taken together, they can increase risk several-fold. When placed in the right environment, an individual who carries such genes will be more likely to develop an eating disorder.

Psychology and Eating Disorders

Certain personality characteristics and psychological problems are common among individuals with eating disorders. In fact, eating disorders frequently co-occur with other psychiatric disorders, such as depression, substance abuse, and anxiety disorders. People with eating disorders tend to have low **self-esteem**. Self-esteem refers to judgments people make and maintain about themselves—a general attitude of approval or disapproval that indicates whether the person thinks he or she is worthy and capable. Self-esteem is shaped by many factors, including how other people respond to you. It can be affected by a history of being teased or ridiculed. It can be influenced by living in a troubled family or having a history of physical or sexual abuse. A high percentage of people with eating disorders have been the victims of rape, incest, molestation, verbal abuse, and neglect.

Eating disorders are rooted in the need for self-control. Those who have eating disorders are often perfectionists who set very high standards for themselves and others. In order to be perfect, they strive to control their bodies and their lives. Everything is viewed as either a success or a failure. Being fat is seen as failure, being thin as success, and being thinner as even better. In spite of their many achievements, those with eating disorders feel inadequate, defective, and worthless. Often, people with eating disorders try to use their relationship with food to gain control over their lives and boost their self-esteem. They believe that controlling their food intake and weight demonstrates their ability to control other aspects of their lives and to solve other problems. Their fixation on food or weight loss and the ability to control their intake and weight help them feel better about themselves. Even if they feel insecure, helpless, or dissatisfied in other areas of life, they are fully in control of their food intake, weight, and body size and, thus, can associate weight control with success. This feeling of control can become addictive.

Society and Eating Disorders

Although genetic and psychological issues may predispose an individual to an eating disorder, it is believed that sociocultural factors are an important trigger for the onset of these disorders. From television and magazines to advertisements and even toys, American society is a culture of thinness. The perfect body is believed to be one that is long, lean, and muscled. Your body is a presentation of who you are to the society. Messages about how we should look are difficult to ignore and can create pressure to achieve this ideal body. Interactions with family members, peer pressure, and the need to fit in often reinforce the importance of achieving the thin ideal and may contribute to abnormal body image and eating disturbances.

Studies have shown that parental pressure to lose weight, family criticism regarding weight, and mothers' concern about their daughters' body size all correlate with the incidence of adolescent eating disturbances.[15] Many people report that they started bulimic behavior in response to family pressure to lose weight. The influence

---

FACT BOX 4.1

Dieting Obsession

We have become a society obsessed with weight and dieting. Americans spend $33 billion a year on weight loss. At any one time, about 45% of adult women and 25% of adult men are trying to lose weight. Ninety-one percent of all women surveyed on a college campus had attempted to control their weight through dieting; 22% said they were always on a diet. Despite all this concern and attention, the number of overweight people has continued to rise and 95% of all dieters gain back the weight they have lost within 1 to 5 years.

of peers is also very strong. If a friend thinks it is good to be thin and is always dieting, you may follow suit. Abnormal eating patterns and practices such as self-induced vomiting for weight control may also be learned from friends. Peer teasing about weight is so significant that it predicts increases in body disturbances and eating problems.

Trying to meet the standards of family, friends, and society in regard to the ideal body may trigger the emergence of an eating disorder. For example, someone who is a perfectionist is likely to try hard to conform to the cultural ideal of the perfect body. In attempting to transform into this ideal, the person may develop an abnormal view of his or her own body, or **body image**. Body image is an important component of self-esteem, especially for women, because we live in a culture that places a great deal of emphasis on the appearance of women's bodies. A poor body image is linked to low self-esteem. Even if they achieve a body weight comparable to that of a fashion model, people with eating disorders may continue to see themselves as fat and strive to lose weight.

DO YOU KNOW SOMEONE WITH AN EATING DISORDER?

Although these disorders are psychological in nature, the physical consequences are very severe. People with eating disorders usually do not recover by themselves. Even if they get better for a period of time, without help, the disorder is likely to return. You cannot provide the

---

FACT BOX 4.2

The Models We Model Ourselves After

- Fashion models are thinner than 98% of American women.

- The average American woman is 5'4" tall and weighs 140 pounds. The average fashion model is 5'11" tall and weighs 117 pounds.

- The average weight of a model is 23% lower than that of an average woman; 40 years ago, the differential was only 8%.

- Medically, the typical fashion model is in a weight range that is below what is recommended for optimal health.

medical and psychological treatment a friend or relative with an eating disorder needs, but that doesn't mean there is nothing you can do. If you suspect that someone you care about has an eating disorder, your goal is to get them to seek professional help. You can do this by alerting a parent, teacher, coach, pastor, school nurse, or other trusted adult about your concerns, or you can confront your friend or relative directly and express your concern.

When confronting someone with an eating disorder, you should be prepared for all possible reactions. Some sufferers may be relieved that someone is concerned and is willing to help, but, more likely, they will be upset, defensive, or angry. They are also likely to be embarrassed and ashamed. People with eating disorders are good at hiding their behaviors and denying that they have a problem, so it may be traumatic for them to learn that someone has discovered their secret. The first reaction of someone confronted about an eating disorder is likely to be to deny that there is a problem. People find protection, comfort, and empowerment in their eating disorder. They may be reluctant to give up these perceived benefits. Seeking treatment may be viewed as an admission of inadequacy and a loss of control. They may also fear the weight gain that would accompany treatment.

When you approach someone about a suspected eating disorder, you need to be firm but supportive and caring. Back up your statements with examples of things you have seen that make you believe your friend has a problem. If you have a lot of evidence, it will be more difficult for the person to deny. When trying to persuade the person to get help, talk about his or her health, relationships, and mood rather than appearance or weight. Unless the illness is viewed as an immediate threat to a person's life, individuals who are 18 years of age or older must make the decision themselves as to whether they will get help. Those under 18 can be forced into treatment by a parent or guardian. However, help is only effective if it is desired. People with eating disorders are likely to refuse help at first. It is therefore important when you approach someone about an eating disorder that you make it clear that you are not forcing him or her to do anything he or she doesn't want to do. Continued encouragement can help some people decide to seek professional help.

HOW CAN EATING DISORDERS BE PREVENTED?

To prevent eating disorders, it is important first to recognize factors that increase risk. These include excessive concerns about body weight, having friends who are preoccupied with weight, teasing from peers about weight and disordered eating, the presence of early eating disorder symptoms, and problems within one's family. There is an association between parental criticism and children's weight preoccupation. Dieting also increases risk. Girls and women who diet are 18 times more likely to develop an eating disorder than those who don't diet.[16] People who have a mother, sister, or friend who diets are also at increased risk. Exposure to media pressure to be thin is also associated with the development of eating disorders.

To prevent eating disorders, it is important to identify individuals who are at risk so they can be targeted for intervention. Parents play an important role. If they arrange an evaluation with a physician and a mental health specialist when the first signs are discovered, a full-blown disorder may be prevented. More widespread interventions to prevent eating disorders should target the elimination of weight-related teasing and criticism from peers and family members. Another important target is the media. If the unrealistically thin body ideal presented by the media could be altered, the incidence of eating disorders would likely decrease. Another approach is education. Lectures given by individuals who are recovering from eating disorders and educational programs offered through schools and communities can help people identify friends and family members who are at risk and persuade those with early symptoms to seek help. Eating disorders are easier to prevent than to cure.

CONNECTIONS

Eating disorders are most common among adolescent women. Men are affected at a much lower rate. All ethnic groups are affected to some extent. Athletes are at particular risk because they are under strong pressure to maintain a body weight that optimizes their performance. Eating disorders are caused by a complex interaction of genetic, psychological, and sociocultural factors. Genes determine the personality traits and other biological factors that predispose people to eating disorders. Psychological problems such as low self-esteem, depression, insecurity, and anxiety further increase risk. Sociocultural factors that reinforce the view of the perfect body as a thin body act as a trigger for the development of an abnormal body image and eating disorders. Pressure from parents or other family members can also influence body image. If you have a friend or family member who you suspect has an eating disorder, you should be caring and supportive while encouraging the person to seek professional help. Preventing eating disorders depends on identifying risk factors and eliminating them, or identifying people who are at risk and targeting them for early intervention.

5

Body Image

Body image can be thought of as the picture of your body that you form in your mind. It is how you perceive and imagine yourself. When you look in the mirror, you compare what you see with what you think you should look like. Your definition of what you think you should look like or wish you would look like is affected by the ideals of your culture and society. How you compare yourself to this ideal influences how you feel about your own body and how satisfied you are with your body image.

What is viewed as an ideal body differs across cultures and has changed throughout history. Paleontological drawings and figurines show women with large breasts and swollen abdomens. Prehistoric Greek, Babylonian, and Egyptian sculptures represent women with large, pregnant abdomens and heavy hips and thighs (Figure 5.1). These images stand in stark contrast to the thin fashion model currently viewed as beautiful in modern American society. The United States today is the fattest society in history, yet women strive to attain the beauty ideal of an extremely thin body. Food is plentiful,

Figure 5.1 In primitive cultures, the ideal female form was very different from the image we see in fashion magazines today. Even in modern times, in places where food is not readily available, the ideal body type is much plumper than that promoted in North America.

yet we yearn to be thin, whereas in cultures where food is scarce and obesity is rare, young women may go to great lengths to gain weight to be attractive.

BODY IMAGE IN DIFFERENT CULTURES

Throughout human history, food shortage has been a constant concern and obesity has been almost nonexistent. As a result, large body size was admired as a symbol of health, prestige, and prosperity. Today, cultures in which the risk of starvation is real continue to view a plump physique with these same positive associations. In many developing nations, big women are considered sexually attractive and beautiful, and plumpness is seen as a sign of fertility, strength, and survival. For example, among the Kipsigis of Kenya, a fatter bride commands a higher dowry. In the Havasupai nation of the American Southwest, fat legs, and, to a lesser extent, fat arms, are considered essential to beauty. Among the Amhara people of Ethiopia, thin hips are undesirable and are referred to by the derogatory term *dog hips*. A cross-cultural survey found that 81% of societies viewed plumpness or "being filled out" as desirable.[17]

Cultural ideals about body size are linked to body image and the incidence of eating disorders. Eating disorders occur in societies where food is abundant and the body ideal is thin. They do not occur where food is scarce and people have to worry about where their next meal is coming from. For example, there is a lower incidence of eating disorders among women living in non-Western, nonindustrialized nations and among certain ethnic minorities in the United States. Immigrants to Western countries are more likely to develop eating disorders than those who remain in their country of origin. As economic changes occur in non-Western societies, the incidence of eating disorders is increasing. They are becoming common clinical problems in young women in high-income Asian societies such as Japan, Hong Kong, Singapore, Taiwan, and the Republic of Korea. They have also appeared in major cities in low-income Asian countries such as China, Malaysia, the Philippines, and Indonesia. They have even been identified in unexpected locations such as India and Africa.

THE CHANGING AMERICAN BODY IDEAL

In the United States, the image of the perfect body has changed over the last century. Many of these changes have followed other trends in society. In the 19th and early 20th centuries, a small waist and full hips were fashionable. Corsets were worn to make the waist small and full skirts and bustles were used to make hips look full. This clothing was not comfortable but it hid flaws and helped make the body better fit the ideal. In order to get the ideal look, women had to change their clothes—not change their bodies.

In the 1920s, some major changes occurred in women's lives and in their fashions. They won the right to vote and it became more common for them to work outside the home. As women moved into the male-dominated workforce, having a less feminine body allowed them to fit in and be taken more seriously. A plump, full figure was associated with being maternal, tied to home and family. Thinness was equated with being sexy, free, and available, and this association helped launch the popularity of the flapper look. The flapper look featured both short hair and short skirts. Flapper styles emphasized a slim figure with small breasts, a slim waist, and narrow hips. Corsets were not worn under the short, loose flapper dresses (Figure 5.2). Now, to have the "in" look, women needed to change their bodies— not just tighten their corsets.

There were a few other events in the 1920s that had a significant impact on how women viewed their bodies. One was an increase in the availability and popularity of ready-made clothes. Before this time, clothes were typically made at home or by a family seamstress, so clothing size was not an issue. The dress was made to fit the body. Mass-production of clothes meant that dresses had to have standard sizes. The body had to fit the dress. This gave women a numerical way to compare themselves to others. There were now women who did not fit within the standard sizing system. If you were a plus size, you knew you did not fit the norm. The 1920s was also the decade when the Miss America Pageant was founded and, for the first time, a large number of young women nationwide systematically made efforts to lower their weight through food restriction and exercise. Dieting for weight loss became popular.

The focus on thinness was less intense in the 1930s. During this time, the Great Depression increased worries about getting

Figure 5.2 The fashion style known as the flapper look (left) freed women's bodies from the discomfort of the corset (right) and led to changes in what was perceived as a desirable body shape. It also encouraged women to diet to achieve the ideal body image.

enough to eat. Also, an increase in immigration brought new people to America. Many of them had suffered hunger throughout their lives, and wanted their children to be plump rather than thin. They saw plumpness as a symbol of their achievement in the New World. In this immigrant culture, fat was a symbol of success and freedom from want. Worries about the lung disease tuberculosis also made thinness undesirable to many. One of the first symptoms of tuberculosis was weight loss, so a child who stayed fat was considered healthy.

In the early 1940s, the United States was focused more on World War II and less on body size. In the 1940s and 1950s, actresses like Jayne Mansfield, Jane Russell, and Marilyn Monroe, who were known for their curves and large breasts, were the ideal. Rather than focusing on thinness, women aspired to have breasts like Marilyn Monroe (Figure 5.3a). In the 1950s, large, lifted, pointy breasts were the beauty standard. Bras began to be mass-produced and exercises to increase bust size were published in magazines. The thinness message, however, had not gone away. *Seventeen* magazine began publication in 1944 to target teens. By 1948, it was publishing articles on dieting and the importance of looking attractive.

The physical standards for women in the 1960s were reflected by the immense popularity of Barbie, a doll introduced in 1959. Barbie's improbable figure—large chest and pinched waist, with hips somewhere in between—was an exaggerated version of the ideal body type of the era. Thin actresses like Audrey Hepburn were favorites and thin fashion models began to gain in popularity. The person who did the most to popularize the waiflike look was British fashion model Twiggy (Figure 5.3b). Twiggy was 5 feet, 7 inches tall and weighed just 91 pounds. Her arrival in the 1960s triggered a downward shift in average sizes for fashion models. As teenage girls tried to achieve the "Twiggy look," dieting increased in popularity. Weight Watchers®, an international organization designed to promote weight management, was founded in 1963; it recruited 500,000 members the first year and grossed $5.5 million in revenue.

In the 1970s, although thin was still in, being fit and toned also became popular. This trend continued into the 1980s and 1990s, with exercise tapes promoting fitness. Today, women are supposed to be thin, but rather than the waif look, a more athletic and toned body is the ideal. The average fashion model today is 5 feet, 8 inches tall and weighs between 108 and 125 pounds. This weight to height ratio puts most models in the underweight category.

THE MEDIA AFFECT YOUR BODY IMAGE

In American society, messages about what the perfect body looks like are constantly delivered by the mass media. Television, movies, magazines, and advertisements show us what society views as a perfect body—the ideal we should strive for. The tall, dark, muscular man gets the girl; the thin, athletic woman gets her

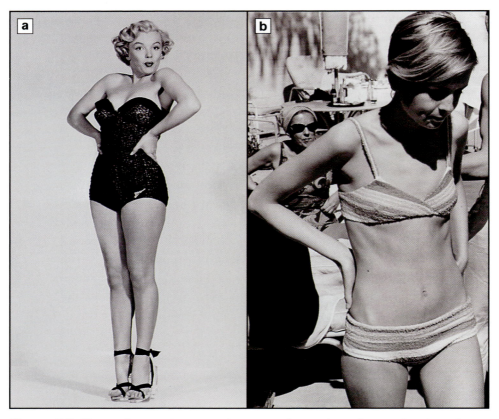

Figure 5.3 The bodies people see on the pages of magazines dictate what they view as the body ideal. In the 1950s, the full-breasted, curvaceous figure of Marilyn Monroe (a) was seen as the perfect body, but in the 1960s, the extremely thin, waiflike Twiggy (b) was at the height of fashion. Although body ideals vary over time, in recent decades, thinness has become more and more important in U.S. society.

man. The most successful movie stars are slim and gorgeous. Thin models show us how the latest fashions should look. All of this adds up to a standard that is very difficult to meet, a standard that is contributing to disturbances in body image and eating behavior. This is illustrated by the fact that as the body dimensions of female models, actresses, and other cultural icons have become thinner over the last several decades, the incidence of eating disorders

FACT BOX 5.1

A Timeline of Weight Consciousness

1900: Stage actress Lillian Russell is considered a beauty ideal, at about 200 pounds.

1920s: Fashion designer Paul Poiret develops the flapper look. Home scales are introduced. Ready-made clothes produced in standard sizes become popular.

1921: The first Miss America beauty pageant is held in Atlantic City, New Jersey.

1950s: Marilyn Monroe epitomizes shifting beauty standards, with a change in focus from weight to large breasts.

1959: Phentermine (Phen), an appetite suppressant that increases the body's metabolism, is approved by the Food and Drug Administration (FDA) to help speed weight loss.

1960s: Twiggy is the leading fashion model. Dieting becomes popular for the masses.

1977: Liquid-protein diets are banned temporarily after three deaths are reported during the 1970s.

1981: Jane Fonda's workout book is an instant best-seller and continues the fitness craze of the 1970s.

1980s: Liposuction is imported from France and approved in the United States. Twenty deaths are reported during its first six years in America.

1983: Singer Karen Carpenter dies at age 32 from anorexia nervosa, bringing eating disorders to widespread attention.

1995: The U.S. Centers for Disease Control and Prevention (CDC) estimates that 5–10 million women have eating disorders.

1997: Diet drugs phentermine and fenfluramine (Phen-fen) are voluntarily taken off the market after being associated with heart valve damage. Tens of thousands of users are at risk.

2000: Despite the nation's obsession with diet and exercise, obesity is on the rise. According to the CDC, obesity affects nearly one in five Americans.

has increased. Another example of the impact the media have on body image and eating disorders is the increase in the rates of body image and eating disturbances seen in the Pacific island of Fiji following the introduction of Western media. Before this, Fiji had had no thin-ideal body images.[15]

YOUR BODY IMAGE

The goal for everyone is to maintain a healthy body image. This means that the mental image you have of your body is accurate and positive. Body image can change with age, mood, environment, and life experiences.

How Body Image Develops

How we feel about our bodies is affected by our experiences as well as changes in our bodies. A child's body image changes as he or she grows to fit with the current body structure. The child absorbs media messages about body size and shape and the attitudes of others toward his or her body and its parts. He or she may develop a body concept that is pleasing and satisfying or one that is unpleasant and shameful. The attitudes of parents have a particularly strong effect on a child's view of an ideal body.

Body image problems are common during the teen years. As teens go through puberty, they experience significant changes in their bodies. These changes occur at different times in different people because everyone develops at a different rate—some faster and some slower. The rate at which teens develop becomes tied to their emotions and how they feel about themselves and their bodies. Some become more self-conscious about their bodies than do their peers. The teen years also bring new social pressures. Insecurity is common as teens struggle to feel socially accepted. Concern about their own development and fitting in with peers puts teens at risk of developing a poor body image and an eating disorder.

Developing and maintaining a healthy body image involves paying attention to your body by practicing good nutrition and including exercise in your lifestyle. It also means accepting and appreciating your body as it is. Having a healthy body image means being realistic about your size based on your family history and realizing that, especially during the adolescent years, weight and body shape can change frequently.

Body Image Problems

Problems with body image usually involve dissatisfaction with one's body and a distortion of one's body image. Dissatisfaction means that you don't like your body or some part of your body. Distortion of body image means that you are unable to judge the size of your

---

FACT BOX 5.2

Dos and Don'ts of a Healthy Body Image

DO

- Accept that bodies come in many shapes and sizes.

- Recognize your positive qualities.

- Remember that you can be your worst critic.

- Explore your internal self, emotionally and spiritually, as well as your external appearance.

- Spend your time and energy enjoying the positive things in your life.

- Be aware of your own weight prejudice. Explore how those feelings may affect your self-esteem.

DON'T

- Let your body define who or what you are.

- Judge others on the basis of appearance, body size, or shape.

- Forget that society changes its ideals of beauty over time.

- Forget that you are not alone in your pursuit of self-acceptance.

- Be afraid to enjoy life.

Adapted from *http://www.mckinley.uiuc.edu/Handouts/bodyimage.html.*

body. People with eating disorders often have distorted body images and do not see themselves as they really are. They may see themselves as fat even if they are not. Often, they equate being thin not only with beauty, but with vitality, success, and intelligence. A desire to achieve these goals is often tied to how they view their bodies and food intake. These problems in body image increase the risk of developing eating disorders. Body image distortion is common in anorexia; individuals with this disorder often insist that their emaciated bodies are not too thin but rather are just right or even slightly plump.

An unhealthy body image can affect your eating habits and health. Because changes in the amount of food you eat can change your body size and shape, people who are unhappy with their bodies may use food and eating patterns as a way to change their bodies to fit a particular image. For some, a weight loss diet that causes them to slim down makes them happier with their bodies, but for others, no amount of dieting will help them feel good about themselves.

CONNECTIONS

Body image is how you perceive and imagine your body. What is viewed as the ideal body differs among cultures. In most developing nations, the female ideal is plumper than it is in Western industrialized societies. In the United States, what is viewed as a perfect body has changed over the last century. Today, the ideal female image is one that is unrealistically thin. This image is seen

FACT BOX 5.3

Do You Really Need to Lose Weight?

There are many people in the United States who are overweight, but there are also an alarming number who just think they are. The majority of women, whether or not they have an eating disorder, think they are bigger than they are. One study reported that 50% of women surveyed thought they were too fat, but only 17% of them were actually overweight.

on television, in magazines, and in the movies. Comparing themselves to this ideal can cause many women to see themselves as too fat and to develop a negative body image. Pressure from family and peers to diet can further distort body image and lead to abnormal eating behaviors and increase the risk of eating disorders. Having a healthy body image means you are accepting and appreciative of your body and realistic about your body size. The most common body image problems include dissatisfaction with your body and distortion, which is the inability to see yourself as you really are. Body image problems can affect eating behavior and increase the risk of eating disorders.

6

A Healthy Body Weight

What we view as the perfect body is often more dependent on what society tells us is beautiful than what medicine tells us is healthy. As a result, many American women strive to attain a body weight that has little relation to what is actually healthy. We know that being too fat is not healthy, but we rarely think about the fact that being too thin also carries health risks.

WHAT IS A HEALTHY BODY WEIGHT?

A healthy body weight is the weight at which your risk of illness and death is lowest. It is the weight that is associated with greatest health and longevity. A healthy body weight for you depends on how much you weigh relative to your height. It also depends on how much body fat you have and where that fat is located on your body.

Weight for Height

The standard currently used to assess body weight for a given height is **body mass index**, or **BMI**. To determine your BMI, divide your weight in kilograms by the square of your height in meters. Or, you can multiply the square of your height in inches by 703, then divide that product by your weight in pounds.

For example, someone who is 6 feet (72 inches) tall and weighs 180 pounds has a body mass index of 24.4 kg/m^2 (180/72^2 x 703). For children and teens, a healthy BMI is one that falls between the 5th and 85th percentiles on the growth charts (see Appendix C). A BMI less than the 5th percentile is considered **underweight**; a BMI between the 85th and 95th percentiles is considered at risk for overweight and a BMI above the 95th percentile is overweight. A healthy BMI for adults falls between 18.5 and 24.9 kg/m^2 (Figure 6.1). In adults, underweight is defined as a BMI of less than 18.5 kg/m^2, **overweight** is defined as a BMI between 25 and 29.9 kg/m^2, and **obese** as a BMI of 30 kg/m^2 or greater. A BMI of 40 kg/m^2 or over is classified as **extreme** or **morbid obesity**.

The average BMI of adults in the United States today is 26.5 kg/m^2. Above a BMI of 25, the risk of obesity-related diseases such as heart disease and diabetes is increased. Health risks are also increased in people with BMIs in the underweight range of less than 18.5; individuals with anorexia nervosa may have a BMI of 16 or less.

BMI is the currently accepted standard for assessing body weight because it correlates well with the amount of body fat an individual has. However, it is not the only measure needed to evaluate the health risks associated with being overweight or obese. People who have a BMI in the overweight range but who consume a healthy diet and exercise regularly may be more fit and consequently have a lower disease risk than someone with a BMI in the healthy range who is sedentary and eats a poor diet. On the other hand, sometimes people have a high BMI but do not have excess body fat. This is often the case with bodybuilders, who may have a high body weight and BMI because their large muscles give them a large amount of **lean body mass**. Their BMI is high but their body fat is in the recommended range, so their health risks are low.

Are you overweight or obese?

The Body Mass Index (BMI) is used to determine whether a person is at a healthy weight, overweight or obese. BMI has some limitations, in that it can overestimate body fat in people who are very muscular and it can underestimate body fat in people who have lost muscle mass, such as many elderly.

Calculating your BMI	Body Mass Index (BMI)	=	$\dfrac{\text{Weight (pounds)}}{\text{Height (inches)}^2}$	x 703

Body Mass Index (BMI) chart

Key ☐ Healthy weight (Below 25) ☐ Overweight (25-29) ■ Obese (30+)

Weight in pounds

Height	120	130	140	150	160	170	180	190	200	210	220	230	240	250
4'6	29	31	34	36	39	41	43	46	48	51	53	56	58	60
4'8	27	29	31	34	36	38	40	43	45	47	49	52	54	56
4'10	25	27	29	31	34	36	38	40	42	44	46	48	50	52
5'0	23	25	27	29	31	33	35	37	39	41	43	45	47	49
5'2	22	24	26	27	29	31	33	35	37	38	40	42	44	46
5'4	21	22	24	26	28	29	31	33	34	36	38	40	41	43
5'6	19	21	23	24	26	27	29	31	32	34	36	37	39	40
5'8	18	20	21	23	24	26	27	29	30	32	34	35	37	38
5'10	17	19	20	22	23	24	26	27	29	30	32	33	35	36
6'0	16	18	19	20	22	23	24	26	27	28	30	31	33	34
6'2	15	17	18	19	21	22	23	24	26	27	28	30	31	32
6'4	15	16	17	18	20	21	22	23	24	26	27	28	29	30
6'6	14	15	16	17	19	20	21	22	23	24	25	27	28	29
6'8	13	14	15	17	18	19	20	21	22	23	24	25	26	28

NOTE: Chart is for adults aged 20 and older.

SOURCE: Office of the Surgeon General   **AP**

Figure 6.1 To determine your BMI range, locate your weight at the top of the scale and your height on the left-hand side. Draw a line down from your weight number and to the right of your height number. The point where the two lines meet within the graph indicates your BMI.

Body Composition

The amount of body fat you have relative to muscle, or body composition, affects your health risks more than your total weight alone. Having too much body fat is associated with an increased risk of many chronic health problems, such as heart disease, cancer, and diabetes. Generally, we refer to the condition of carrying excess fat as being overweight. But it is really excess fat and not weight that can affect health.

What is considered a healthy amount of body fat varies with age and gender. Babies and children have a greater percentage of body fat than adults do, and their body composition changes as they grow. During adolescence, the body composition of males and females begins to differ—females gain proportionately more fat and males gain more muscle mass. As adults, women continue to have more stored body fat than men do. A healthy level of body fat for a young adult female is between 20 and 30% of total weight; for young adult males, it is between 12 and 20%.[4] As people get older, lean body mass decreases and their percentage of body fat increases.

Your health is the most important criterion for determining how much you should weigh and how much body fat you should carry. You need enough fat to perform essential functions such as insulating your body, providing energy reserves, and supporting normal hormonal activity, but not so much that it impairs health. People who live and work in cold climates may benefit from extra body fat to prevent heat loss. Athletes who participate in sports such as distance running or cycling may benefit from a lower percentage of body fat. For some male athletes, an ideal body fat level is only 5 to 10% and for women 15 to 20%. In people with anorexia nervosa, body fat percentage drops so low that body temperature cannot be maintained, there is no cushioning to protect other organs and tissues, and hormonal activity is abnormal.

MEASURING BODY FAT

The amount of body fat you have can be measured in a number of ways. One of the easiest methods measures skinfold thicknesses. By measuring the thickness of the skin and the underlying fat layer with a caliper, the amount of **subcutaneous fat**—that is, the fat under the skin, is estimated. It is assumed that subcutaneous fat

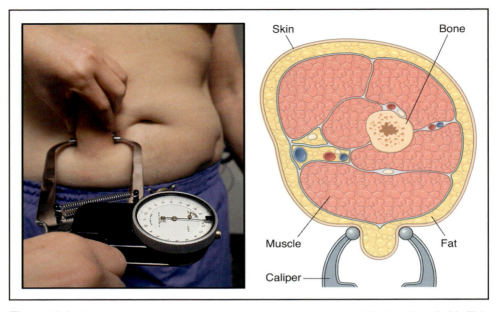

Figure 6.2 Body fat is measured using an instrument called a skinfold caliper (left). This cross-section of an arm (right) illustrates the location of the fat under the skin and how this fat layer is measured.

is representative of the total body fat (Figure 6.2). Measurements of thickness are taken at one or more body locations and mathematical equations are then used to estimate the percentage of body fat. A more accurate assessment of body fat percentage can be done using either water or air displacement. Underwater weighing uses the difference between an individual's weight on land and in the water to determine body volume. The percentage of body fat can then be determined using standardized equations. A similar determination can be made by using an air-filled chamber called a BOD POD to determine air displacement. Body composition can also be determined by measuring the rate at which a mild electrical current flows through the body; this technique is called bioelectric impedance. A painless electrical current is directed through the body with a handheld meter or a specially designed scale. Because fat is a poor conductor of electricity, the higher the percentage of body fat, the greater the resistance to current flow and the slower the rate of current flow. Although impedance measures can be accurate, the results are affected by changes in body water caused by factors such as water loss in sweat, a full GI tract, or a full bladder. In research settings, body fat is often assessed by the principle of dilution. Because water is present primarily in lean tissue and not in fat, a detectable water-soluble substance can be ingested or injected into the bloodstream and allowed to mix with the water throughout the body. The concentration of this substance in a sample of body fluid can then be measured and the extent to which it has been diluted used to calculate the amount of lean tissue. A variety of sophisticated imaging techniques such as dual-energy X-ray absorptiometry (DEXA), CT scans (computerized axial tomography), and magnetic resonance imaging (MRI) can also be used to assess the amount and location of body fat. These require expensive equipment and are only used for research investigations.

Are You an Apple or a Pear?

Not all body fat is the same when it comes to health. When excess body fat is located under the skin (subcutaneous fat), it carries less risk than when the excess fat is deposited around the internal organs (**visceral fat**). An increase in visceral fat is associated with a higher incidence of chronic diseases such as heart disease and diabetes. Where an individual deposits body fat is determined primarily by genetics, but gender, age, and lifestyle also influence where fat is stored. Visceral fat storage is more common in men than in women. After menopause, however, visceral fat increases in women. Stress, tobacco use, and alcohol consumption predispose people to visceral fat deposition, whereas activity reduces it.

Distinguishing the relative amounts of visceral and subcutaneous fat requires sophisticated imaging techniques, but, in general, excess fat around and above the waist is predominantly visceral fat, whereas fat in the hips and lower body is subcutaneous. Therefore, people with pear-shaped bodies, who carry their extra fat below the waist, have more subcutaneous fat and a lower risk for health problems. Those who have more visceral fat have apple-shaped bodies and are at greater risk (Figure 6.3). The amount of visceral fat an individual carries can be estimated by measuring his or her waist circumference. For males, a BMI of 25 to 34.9 kg/m^2 and a waist circumference greater than 40 inches increases the risk of weight-related diseases such as diabetes and heart disease. For females in this BMI range, a waist circumference of greater than 35 inches increases risks.

THE RISKS OF BEING OVERWEIGHT

Excess stored body fat increases the incidence of some medical problems and the risk of others. It is estimated that 300,000 people die each year from obesity-related diseases.[18] Being overweight also can create psychological and social problems.

Being Overweight Can Be Bad for Your Health

Carrying excess body fat increases the risk of developing high blood pressure, atherosclerosis, high blood cholesterol, diabetes, stroke, gallbladder disease, arthritis, sleep disorders, respiratory problems, and cancers of the breast, uterus, prostate, and colon. Obesity can also increase the incidence and severity of infectious disease and has been linked to poor wound healing and surgical complications. The health risks associated with obesity are greater in people who gained their excess weight at a young age and have remained overweight throughout life. Obesity also increases pregnancy risks for both the mother and child.

FACT BOX 6.1

An Obesity Epidemic

The number of obese people in the United States has been steadily increasing for the last two decades. Today, more than 30% of adults are obese. If this trend continues at its current rate, 39% of American adults will be obese by 2008. Among children and adolescents, 15% are too fat; this is an increase of 36% in a decade.

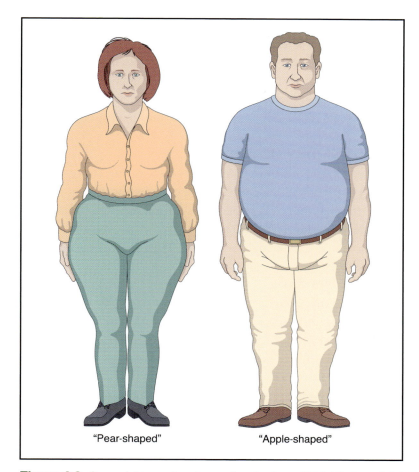

"Pear-shaped"   "Apple-shaped"

Figure 6.3 Overweight people who are "apple-shaped" (right) deposit fat in the abdominal region, around body organs, and are at a greater risk of heart disease and diabetes. People who are "pear-shaped" (left) carry their fat under the skin in the hips and thighs, which presents fewer health risks.

Being Overweight Can Lead to Discrimination

In addition to medical problems, psychological and social problems are associated with being overweight. Overweight children are often teased and ostracized. They frequently find themselves isolated socially from their peers. Obese adolescents and adults may experience discrimination in college admissions and in the job market. Social embarrassment occurs on a daily basis for those who are too large to fit into the seats in movie theaters or on airplanes. The physical health risks of obesity may not show up as disease for years, but the psychological and social problems experienced by the obese are felt every day. Obese individuals of all ages are more likely to experience depression, a negative self-image, and feelings of inadequacy.

IS BEING SKINNY HEALTHY?

Some fat storage is essential. Individuals who have little stored fat have a greater risk for illness than those whose body fat is within the normal range. However, the health implications for someone who is naturally on the lean side are very different from the health problems seen in someone who is starving due to a food shortage or an eating disorder.

Natural Leanness

Research has suggested that being on the low side of the body weight standard may reduce the risk of diabetes, and may even increase longevity. Despite the health advantages of leanness, some body fat is essential to insulate the body and to act as a reserve for periods of illness. People with little energy reserves have a disadvantage when battling a medical condition such as cancer, which causes wasting and malnutrition. Therefore, statistically, a low body weight is associated with an increased risk of early death.

Starvation

The health risks of low body fat are much greater when that low body fat is caused by starvation. Starvation may be due to a food shortage, an illness, or intentional deprivation due to an eating disorder. At first, starvation causes a decrease in the amount of body fat, but as energy restriction continues, body protein is also lost and growth rate decreases. Starvation in children can lead to stunted growth and impaired mental development. Low body fat also makes it hard for a person to tolerate cold. As starvation progresses, its victims become weak, find it difficult to concentrate, and may have trouble sleeping. Metabolic rate slows to decrease energy expenditure. In females, estrogen levels drop and abnormalities in the menstrual cycle occur.

Substantial reductions in body weight have been shown to decrease the ability of the immune system to fight disease, increasing the risk of infection. In the final stages of starvation, the person is inactive, apathetic, and withdraws from life. Conditions such as electrolyte imbalances, dehydration, edema, cardiac abnormalities, and infection eventually become life-threatening.

WHAT DETERMINES HOW MUCH YOU WEIGH?

Many people are unhappy with their body weight. For some, this is because they are too thin, but most are dissatisfied because they are too fat. Whether you are happy with what you weigh or not, in most people, body fat and weight remain remarkably constant over long periods despite day-to-day fluctuations in food intake and activity level. One reason for this is that body weight is internally regulated to stay at a particular level. Another reason is related to environmental and lifestyle factors that influence typical food intake and exercise patterns.

Energy Balance

The principle of energy balance states that when the number of calories you eat equals the number of calories you burn, your weight will remain stable. We consume calories in food and beverages. We burn calories to stay alive, digest and absorb food, and perform activity. Being in energy balance means that the calories you eat are equal to the calories you expend. It does not mean that you are at a healthy weight. You can be in energy balance when you are overweight, underweight, or at a healthy weight. However, to lose or gain weight, energy intake needs to be out of balance with expenditure. When you take in more energy than you use, the extra energy is stored, mostly as fat, and your weight increases. When energy expenditure exceeds energy intake, the body uses stored energy to meet needs and weight decreases.

How Is Energy Balance Regulated?

Have you ever known someone who never gains an ounce no matter how much he or she eats, or someone who seems to eat nothing but is still overweight? The reason for this is related to the genetic predisposition we inherit from our parents. Our bodies tend to be set at a specific weight, and this setting is difficult to change. When energy intake or activity level changes, the body works to minimize changes in weight or fat. For example, when you lose weight, regardless of whether you are lean or obese at the outset, your body generates signals to decrease energy output and increase energy intake to return your weight to its set point.

Your genes carry the information that regulates energy balance, body size, and body shape and, therefore, the set point for body fat. Because this information is inherited from your parents, if one or both of your parents are obese, your risk of becoming obese is increased. There is no single gene that determines your body size; rather, there are a host of genes, often referred to as "obesity genes," involved in the regulation of body weight. The proteins made by obesity genes are often involved in sending signals about energy intake and levels of fat stores to the brain. The brain monitors, integrates, and organizes these signals and then sends messages to other parts of the body to control food intake and energy expenditure. When a gene involved in the regulation of body weight is defective, the protein for which it codes is not made or is made incorrectly. The signals to decrease food intake and/or increase energy expenditure are therefore not received, and weight gain results. Most human obesity is not likely to be due to a single abnormal gene but rather to variations in many genes that interact with one another and the environment to regulate body shape and size as well as energy intake and expenditure.

Despite the many genes that are involved in controlling body weight, the mechanisms that hold body weight around a particular set point are not absolute. Changes in physiological circumstances do cause changes at the level at which body weight is maintained, usually increasing it over time. For example, body weight increases in most

FACT BOX 6.2

Stored Fat Keeps You Going

The average man who weighs 70 kilograms (154 pounds) stores about 115,000 Calories in his adipose (fat) tissue. Someone would need to do aerobics for 9-1/2 days without stopping to achieve the same amount of energy.

adults between the ages of 30 and 60, and after childbearing, most women return to a weight that is one to two pounds higher than their pre-pregnancy weight. This suggests that the mechanisms that keep us from losing weight are stronger than those that prevent weight gain.

How Lifestyle Affects Body Weight

The typical American lifestyle today promotes excess food intake and discourages physical activity. We are constantly exposed to an abundance of high-calorie, high-fat, high-sugar foods. Bigger is marketed to us as a good value, so we order larger burgers and supersized drinks. Exercise is often unnecessary because modern conveniences reduce the energy required for many of the activities of daily living. Even our leisure time is often spent in sedentary fashion in front of the television or computer. Scientists believe this lifestyle is a major reason for the growing number of obese people in the United States.

Genes and Environment Interact

Body weight is determined by the interaction between our genetic tendencies and the environmental factors that influence how much we eat and exercise. Thus, an individual with parents of normal

---

FACT BOX 6.3

Supersizing: Good Value or Bad Idea?

For only 39 cents extra, you can supersize that! Americans' love of a bargain is contributing to their supersized waistlines. In 1954, when the McDonald brothers sold their first hamburger, it weighed 1.6 ounces. Today, burgers can weigh up to 8 ounces. In 1955, an order of fries weighed 2.5 ounces—a supersized order today is almost 3 times that. Restaurants have capitalized on our love of a good value. Since food is only a small percentage of what it costs a restaurant to operate, giving customers more food is a good way to increase overall sales. But it may be a bad idea for you when it comes to managing your weight and health.

Source: Young, L., and M. Nestle. "Expanding portion sizes in the U.S. marketplace: Implications for nutrition counseling." *Journal of the American Dietetic Association* 103 (2003): 231–234.

weight who indulges in supersized portions of fast food and does not engage in any physical activity can find him- or herself at an unhealthy level of body fat. On the other hand, someone with obese parents can avoid becoming overweight by exercising regularly and eating moderately. Having an eating disorder can also override your genetically programmed level of body fat. For example, in someone who has anorexia nervosa, psychological problems prevail over the regulatory mechanisms that protect against weight loss, so the person is able to severely restrict his or her food intake. Likewise, a binge eater may be overweight due to overconsumption, even if his or her parents are lean.

CONNECTIONS

A healthy body weight is associated with health and longevity. The current standard for assessing body weight is body mass index (BMI). In most people with a BMI above the healthy range, the risk of chronic diseases such as heart disease, diabetes, and respiratory problems is increased. The amount of body fat you have relative to lean tissue affects health risks more than body weight itself. BMI correlates with the amount of body fat, but a more accurate assessment of body composition can be obtained using techniques such as skinfold thickness, underwater weighing, or bioelectric impedance. The distribution of body fat also affects health risks. Excess visceral fat, which is located around the internal organs in the abdomen, increases health risks more than excess subcutaneous fat, which is generally concentrated around the hips. Excess body fat is associated with an increase in chronic diseases as well as an increased incidence of infections, poor wound healing, and surgical complications. Obesity also contributes to psychological and social problems. People who are naturally lean may have some health advantages, but they have little body reserves on which to draw in the event of a serious illness. Leanness due to starvation can impair immune function, slow growth, and, if it is severe enough, can even be fatal. Body weight is determined by the interaction between genes that regulate body size and shape and environmental factors that influence how much you eat and how much you exercise.

7

Anorexia Nervosa

I cooked dinner for my family tonight using a new recipe I found on the Internet. I even made a chocolate cake for dessert. I love to cook, but I mustn't taste—not one bite. I didn't even lick the spoon from the cake frosting. I was excited to have my parents and brother try the new recipe and served them heaping portions. I took only a very small amount for myself, saying that I had nibbled too much while cooking. I pushed the food around on my plate so Mom wouldn't notice that I only ate a few bites of chicken and some rice. My breakfast today was a cup of herbal tea, and for lunch, I had a few leaves of lettuce. I made it through another day in control.

The scale says I have lost 40 pounds but I still look fat. I must keep losing weight. I hate my body and wish I could be thin and attractive like the other girls at school. Then I would be popular. I will keep up my routine of sit-ups every morning and 5-mile runs after school. I'm a little worried because I am tired and cold all the time at school, which makes it hard to concentrate. I am studying extra at home to make sure I keep my perfect straight-A grades. I haven't had my period in three months and I have little hairs growing all over my body. I lie awake at night worrying that I might lose control and eat too much.

This is a snapshot of anorexia nervosa. It shows us a person who is obsessed with food, yet eats next to nothing. She is beginning to experience physical symptoms, such as a lack of menstrual periods and fine hair growth all over her body, that are typical of anorexia. She fears losing control over her food intake and becoming fat. She works hard to hide the fact that she is not eating from family and friends. The discipline required to restrict food intake or exercise excessively may at first be a source of pride and pleasure for the person with anorexia. As time passes, these accomplishments may be overshadowed by the physiological changes caused by the starvation of anorexia.

WHAT IS ANOREXIA NERVOSA?

Anorexia means "lack of appetite," but in the case of the eating disorder anorexia nervosa, it is a desire to be thin, rather than a lack of appetite, that causes individuals to decrease their food intake. Anorexia nervosa was first recognized in the second half of the 19th century by physicians in both France and England. The characteristics they described over a century ago still apply to the syndrome today: severe weight loss, **amenorrhea**, constipation, and restlessness with no evidence of an underlying physiological disease. At the time anorexia was first described, the first step in its diagnosis was to distinguish it from tuberculosis, which also causes extreme wasting. Even today, a medical examination must rule out other diseases that cause weight loss before a doctor can diagnose anorexia.

Despite the fact that anorexia has been known since the 1870s, it was given little attention until the 1960s, when psychiatrist Hilde Bruch began to study patients with this disorder. Dr. Bruch recognized that a relentless pursuit of thinness and disturbances in body image were components of anorexia. Today, anorexia nervosa affects 0.5 to 3.7% of American women at some point in their lifetime.[11] There is a 5% death rate in the first two years, and this can reach 20% if the sufferers are not treated.[19]

CHARACTERISTICS OF ANOREXIA

Anorexia nervosa most frequently develops during adolescence; it is most common in women between 13 and 25 years of age and is rare among older women; the average age of onset is 17 years. Anorexia is more likely to occur in those whose appearance and body size is the focus of their careers, such as dancers, actors, models, flight attendants, jockeys, gymnasts, and runners. It occurs at a much lower frequency in men than women.

Anorexia is a psychological disorder that has a behavioral component and physical and nutritional consequences that can

---

FACT BOX 7.1

What Do These Women Have in Common?

Jane Fonda

Tracey Gold

Jamie-Lynn Discala

Sally Field

Carey Otis

Paula Abdul

Victoria Beckham

Princess Diana

Justine Bateman

Joan Rivers

Anne Murray

The Barbi Twins

Leila Pahlavi

Whitney Houston

Courtney Thorne-Smith

Amy Heckerling

Barbara Niven

Karen Carpenter

Cathy Rigby

ANSWER: They are all celebrities who have struggled with eating disorders.

be life-threatening. Ways to tell if someone has anorexia include psychological, behavioral, and physical considerations (Table 7.1). Signs that support a diagnosis of anorexia include a refusal to maintain body weight at or above a minimally normal weight for age and height, an intense fear of gaining weight even when the person is underweight, disturbances in how body weight and shape are perceived, and abnormalities in the menstrual cycle (for women).[20] There are two subtypes of anorexia, referred to as the "restricting type" and the "binge-eating/purging type." Those who have the restricting type limit their food intake but do not

Table 7.1 Diagnostic Criteria of Anorexia Nervosa

- Refusal to maintain body weight at or above 85% of normal weight for age and height.

- Intense fear of gaining weight or becoming fat, even when underweight.

- Disturbance in the way body weight or shape is perceived, undue influence of body weight or shape on self-evaluation, or denial of the seriousness of the current low body weight.

- Absence of at least three consecutive menstrual cycles without other known cause.

Types:
- Restricting type—The person does not regularly engage in binge-eating or purging behavior.

- Binge-eating/purging type—The person regularly engages in binge-eating or purging behavior.

regularly engage in binge-eating or purging behavior as those who have the binge-eating/purging type do.

Psychological Disturbances

The psychological component of anorexia nervosa revolves around an overwhelming fear of gaining weight, even in people who are already underweight. It is not uncommon for individuals with anorexia to feel that they would rather be dead than fat. Anorexia is also characterized by a distorted body image that prevents individuals from seeing themselves as underweight even when they are dangerously thin. People with this disorder may use body weight and shape as a means of self-evaluation: "If I weren't so fat, then everyone would like and respect me and I wouldn't have other problems." However, no matter how much weight they lose, they do not gain the self-respect, inner assurance, or happiness they seek. Therefore, they continue to restrict their food intake, overexercise, or use other purging behaviors to help them lose weight.

The typical psychological profile of an anorexic describes a young female who is well behaved, eager to please, and needs no special attention from parents or teachers. Children and adolescents with anorexia are usually described as compliant and helpful children. But underneath this pleasing facade, they are frightened, introverted, and have trouble establishing relationships with their peers. They have a poor opinion of themselves, and this low self-esteem leads them to depend on the opinions of others to feel good about themselves. People with anorexia are also perfectionists. Their perfectionism causes them to expect better performance from themselves and others than is required for a given situation. This can be seen in the extreme importance they place on doing well in school and in sports, on looking great, and on being popular. Perfectionism is so common in anorexics that it is considered a risk factor for the disorder. Despite this drive for perfection in every aspect of their lives, individuals with anorexia are extremely critical of themselves and do not believe they deserve attention.

Other psychological symptoms that are common in anorexia include depressed mood, irritability, social withdrawal, loss of sexual drive, preoccupation with food, obsessive thoughts and behaviors, and, eventually, reduced alertness and concentration. Many of these symptoms are not unique to anorexia; they are common in anyone who is in a state of semi-starvation for any reason. For example, men who participated in a research study that restricted their food intake for six months experienced depression, irritability, anger, apathy, mood swings, and a decreased sex drive. Many became preoccupied with food. It dominated their thoughts, and some hoarded food and ate in a ritualized fashion. Binge eating also occurred in some men who had no previous history of disordered eating.[21]

The psychological aspects of anorexics who only restrict food intake to lose weight are different from those of anorexics who also binge and use purging techniques such as self-induced vomiting to lose weight. Those with the restricting type of anorexia are obsessive, socially inhibited, compliant, and emotionally restrained. Those with binge-eating/purging anorexia have a more impulsive and extroverted personality style, more similar to the personality traits of people who have bulimia nervosa. Those who have the binge-eating/purging type of anorexia tend to have been overweight or obese in childhood and more often come from families with a history of obesity. They are also likely to display other impulsive behavior such as alcohol and drug abuse, stealing, and self-mutilation.

Problems within the family can contribute to the psychological characteristics of individuals with anorexia. The families of anorexics often appear ideal on the outside; the daughters receive plenty of educational and recreational opportunities and emotional attention. But a closer look at the family of someone who has anorexia may reveal that family members do not communicate well and are often excessively concerned with how things will look to outsiders. Mothers of anorexics are often overly intrusive and leave their daughters little privacy. In some cases, the mother may have turned to the daughter with her problems, leaving the daughter feeling as if she has nowhere to go with her own. This overbearing family leaves the child little room to develop independence, and emotional problems arise from separation anxiety and difficulties with identity.

Anorexia often manifests itself at times in life when more independence is expected, such as during adolescence. As the disease progresses and dieting becomes more important, people with anorexia will withdraw from friends and concentrate on study or work. When others try to change their behavior, they become angry and will use deception and manipulation to prevent the change. As the illness becomes more long-term, the anorexic becomes more dependent on family or therapists and more restricted in his or her interests.

Behavioral Component

The behavioral component of anorexia is characterized by what Hilde Bruch described as the "relentless pursuit of thinness." People with anorexia are obsessed with their body weight, checking it repeatedly. In order to achieve thinness, they may engage in behaviors such as self-starvation and abnormal food consumption patterns, intense and compulsive exercise, or purging by means of self-induced vomiting and abuse of laxatives, enemas, and diuretics.

The most obvious behavioral component of anorexia nervosa is a restriction in food intake. Food and eating becomes an obsession. In addition to restricting the total amount of food they eat, anorexics develop personal diet rituals, limiting certain foods and eating foods in specific ways. For example, they may insist on having dinner at a particular time and refuse to eat after that time, or they may have to have food arranged in a certain way on their plates. At the table, they often cut their food into tiny pieces, chew excessively, and eat very slowly. They may consume large quantities of liquids or may excessively restrict their liquid intake. They may have a specific plate that they use and only eat foods in a particular order or in certain combinations. They find ways to avoid meals. For example, they may consistently be late in the morning so they can skip breakfast. They may participate in clubs or sports activities that make it easy for them to skip lunch and avoid having dinner with the family. If they are forced to share food with others, they pick at their food and push it around on the plate. They may take small bites of low-calorie foods like lettuce or apples and chew them hundreds of times to avoid swallowing. They may also secretly dispose of food. Often, the conflicts that develop about eating cause people with anorexia to eat separately from their families and friends.

The foods anorexics do eat frequently depend on diet fads and misconceptions of the times. In the 1960s, anorexic patients avoided simple sugars and carbohydrates; in the 1980s and 1990s, fatty foods and red meat were avoided and many anorexics adopted vegetarian diets. Foods that anorexics commonly allow themselves to eat today are low-calorie products, high-fiber products, and vitamin supplements.

Although anorexics do not consume very much food, they are preoccupied with food. They may spend an enormous amount of time thinking about food, talking about food, and preparing food for others. They may spend a lot of time reading recipes and cookbooks and enter cooking and recipe development contests. They may insist on shopping, cooking, and serving food for others. They take on the role of planning and preparing family meals, although they eat little or nothing themselves. Some may try to impose their restrictive diet on others. For example, the failure of a small child to thrive may be due to an anorexic mother who limits the food intake of her children.

Another behavior that is typical of anorexia is hyperactivity and overactivity. This is in contrast to the decrease in activity and fatigue characteristic of other starvation states associated with weight loss. Many anorexics exercise excessively to burn calories. Sometimes the activity is surreptitious, such as going up and down stairs repeatedly or getting off the bus a few stops too early. For others, the activity takes the form of strenuous physical activity. The sufferer may become a fanatical athlete. Exercise is typically done alone and is performed as a rigid routine. The person feels guilty if he or she cannot exercise. The person may link exercise and eating, so a certain amount of exercise earns the anorexic the right to eat, and if he or she eats too much, a price must be paid by adding extra exercise. Anorexics may wake early so they can exercise for several hours before the rest of the family gets up. Those who use exercise to increase energy expenditure do not stop when they are tired; instead, they exercise compulsively beyond reasonable endurance. In addition to the planned exercise, late in the illness, patients may display a persistent restlessness. This restlessness is hypothesized to be related to a fall in core body temperature. The involuntary activity is the body's way of trying to warm up. This overactive restlessness continues until the patient's condition has deteriorated so much that he or she is simply too weak to keep it up.

Purging is another behavior seen in some anorexics. Scientists estimate that about half of the people with anorexia use purging as a means of weight control. In these patients, vomiting, laxatives, enemas, and diuretics are used in addition to food restriction to further weight loss. Purging is used when the patient feels he or she has lost control and eaten too much. Typically, however, these "binges" are subjective, because they do not contain an excessive amount of food or calories. Purging behaviors are particularly serious because they cause additional physical damage. For example, vomiting brings acid into the mouth and esophagus, where it promotes tooth decay and can cause mouth sores and inflammation. Vomiting, laxatives, and diuretics can all cause dehydration and electrolyte imbalances.

Physical Effects of Anorexia

The most obvious physical and nutritional consequence of anorexia is dramatic weight loss (Figure 7.1). By definition, anorexia is characterized by weight loss to a level that is at or below 85% of normal weight for age and height. The insufficient energy intake and loss of body fat lead to abnormalities in hormone levels and other symptoms of starvation.

Initial weight loss is due mostly to lost fat. With severe energy restriction, liver glycogen stores are depleted and carbohydrates are no longer available to break down fat completely. As a result, ketone

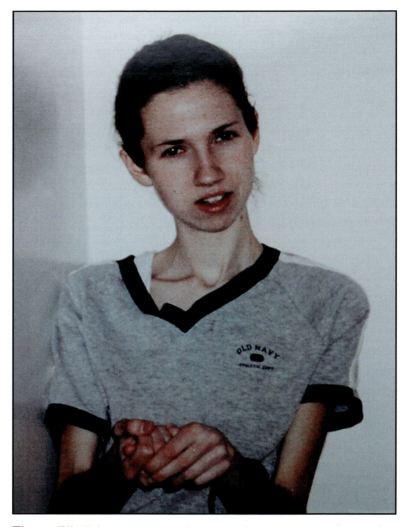

Figure 7.1 This young woman has anorexia nervosa—a serious eating disorder characterized by extreme weight loss. An anorexic usually sees him- or herself as fat, even when the body is grossly emaciated, as seen here.

bodies are formed. If ketone levels build up too high, they can change the acidity in the blood. An outward sign of elevated ketone level is a sweet (acetone) smell on the breath. As the body adapts to starvation, metabolic pathways that synthesize glucose from amino acids are stimulated. This leads to protein breakdown and loss of water from compartments between cells, resulting in electrolyte imbalances and other problems with body metabolism.

As weight loss becomes severe, symptoms of starvation begin to appear. Fat stores are depleted, muscle wasting occurs, and growth decreases. As anorexia progresses, its victims become weak and find it difficult to concentrate. They may have trouble sleeping and the lack of fat padding may make it painful even to sit. Metabolic rate slows, lowering body temperature and energy expenditure. The reduction in insulating body fat leads to cold intolerance, so the anorexic patient bundles up in extra layers of clothing to stay warm.

In females, estrogen levels drop and abnormalities occur in the menstrual cycle (amenorrhea). Girls with anorexia often experience a delayed onset of their first menstrual period. Women with anorexia have infrequent or absent menstrual periods. Although

FACT BOX 7.2

The Fear and Fascination of Starvation

Food is a basic human need. Fear of starvation and anxiety about weight loss are basic human emotions that have evolved in all of us. As a result, food and the lack of it has played a central role throughout human history. Lack of food has been the cause of warfare and has been used as a weapon of war. Hunger and starvation have defeated more armies than bullets or bombs. Intentional starvation has also been used as a weapon. Hunger strikes have been used repeatedly to protest imprisonment or unjust authority. Perhaps the best known are the hunger strikes of Mohandas "Mahatma" Gandhi (1869–1948) during his struggle for the independence of India. Fear of hunger is so great that anyone who voluntarily goes without food for political or other causes inspires admiration and awe. People with anorexia who starve themselves arouse curiosity and fascination and draw power from overcoming this most basic of human fears.

loss of body fat contributes to amenorrhea, other factors are also involved because, in some women, amenorrhea occurs before there has been significant weight loss and persists even after weight is regained. Hormonal changes affect sexual maturation and can have long-term effects on bone density. Amenorrhea, decreased body weight and fat, and low calcium and vitamin D intake all contribute to decreased bone formation, increased bone loss, and a greater risk of osteoporosis. Obviously, amenorrhea is not a possible symptom of anorexia in males, but male reproduction is also affected because testosterone levels decrease.

As weight loss continues, virtually no organ system is left unaffected. Heart rate may slow or become irregular and blood pressure may drop. The movement and emptying of food through the digestive tract slow and the incidence of peptic ulcers increases. Constipation is common, and pancreatitis (inflammation of the pancreas) may occur. In those who vomit frequently, the stomach acid brought into the mouth damages tooth enamel and promotes tooth decay. Kidney damage may occur due to dehydration. The skin may become dry and brittle due to fatty acid deficiency. Hair

---

FACT BOX 7.3

Warning Signs of Anorexia: Are You at Risk?

- Have you lost a significant amount of weight?

- Do you continue to diet even though you are thin?

- Do you feel fat, even after losing weight?

- Are you afraid of gaining weight?

- Has your monthly menstrual period stopped?

- Are you preoccupied with food, calories, nutrition, and/or cooking?

- Do you exercise compulsively?

- Do you binge and purge?

on the head may become dry, thin, and brittle, and there may be abnormal hair growth on other parts of the body. This fine hair growing all over the body is called **lanugo hair**. The risk of infection increases because immune function is compromised.

In the final stages of starvation, patients suffer from electrolyte imbalances, dehydration, edema, cardiac abnormalities, absence of ketones due to fat-store depletion, and finally infection, which further increases the body's nutritional needs. Organs shrink because they lack nutrients and can no longer perform essential functions. Heartbeat is irregular and can lead to cardiac arrest.

TREATING ANOREXIA NERVOSA

The goal of treatment for anorexia nervosa is to help resolve the psychological and behavioral problems while also providing for physical and nutritional rehabilitation (Figure 7.2). Early treatment of anorexia is important because starvation may cause irreversible damage. Ideally, the treatment of eating disorders involves a multidisciplinary approach. The treatment team should include a psychiatrist (a medical doctor) trained in the assessment, treatment, and medical management of people with eating disorders; a psychologist experienced in the group and individual psychotherapy of eating disorders; a nutritionist familiar with the medical nutrition therapy needed by anorexic patients; a social worker experienced in working with the families of patients with eating disorders; an occupational therapist skilled in the psychosocial rehabilitation of patients with eating disorders; and nurses experienced in dealing with the medical and psychiatric needs of eating disorder patients. Each of these practitioners needs to attempt to build a relationship of mutual trust and respect with the patient that will serve as a basis for successful treatment.

Guidelines for the treatment of patients with eating disorders have been outlined by the American Psychiatric Association.[11] The first step in treatment is to determine if the patient needs to be hospitalized or if he or she can be treated as an outpatient. This decision is based on the psychiatric, behavioral, and general physiological condition of the patient. If the person has symptoms that are life-threatening, hospitalization

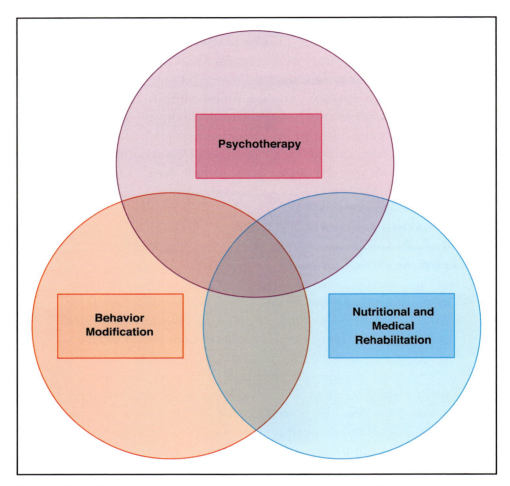

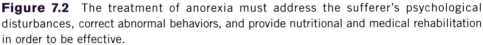

Figure 7.2 The treatment of anorexia must address the sufferer's psychological disturbances, correct abnormal behaviors, and provide nutritional and medical rehabilitation in order to be effective.

is essential. Hospitalization is also the best option for patients who have continued to restrict food intake and lose weight despite outpatient treatment and for those who have other conditions, such as infections or psychiatric problems, that put them at added risk.

The principles involved in the treatment of anorexia nervosa include interrupting abnormal behaviors, treating conditions that occur along with the anorexia, and helping patients learn to think differently about the value of weight loss or body shape change. The goals of treatment are to have the patient regain enough weight so that menstruation resumes in females and hormones return to normal levels in males, and to resume normal physical and sexual growth and development. The patient's eating disorder symptoms and behaviors, general medical condition, and psychiatric status should be continuously monitored and assessed. Treatment may need to be ongoing in order to prevent relapse.

Psychosocial Treatment

Eating disorders are psychological conditions, so psychiatric management is the foundation of the treatment of anorexia. This psychiatric care should be coordinated with other types of clinical care and is not usually begun until the patient is medically stable and weight gain has started.

The goal of therapy is to help patients 1) understand their need for nutritional and physical rehabilitation, 2) change the behaviors related to their weight restriction, 3) improve their interpersonal and social functioning, and 4) address underlying psychological conflicts that are reflected in their eating disorder. The therapy should be individualized to meet the patients' needs based on an understanding of their personal conflicts, cognitive development, and psychological defenses. A patient's motivation to change his or her behaviors needs to be assessed and addressed. The presence of other psychiatric disorders may also need to be considered if successful treatment is to help stop abnormal behaviors and prepare the patient to go back into society.

Group therapy is sometimes used in conjunction with other treatments for anorexia nervosa. However, it is important that the group therapy not become a contest in which patients compete to see who can be the thinnest or the sickest. There is also a risk in group therapy that a recovering patient may become demoralized by seeing a lack of progress in the recovery of other patients in the group.

Because familial relationships may contribute to the cause and maintenance of eating disorders, family or couples psychotherapy may be required. Family support is essential for successful treatment, and family members may also need counseling and therapy to change their interactions with the patient and to deal with guilt that may arise from having a sick family member.

Treatment must be ongoing for at least a year because of the enduring nature of many of the underlying psychological aspects of anorexia nervosa. The need for support during recovery may extend psychological treatment to five or more years.

Medical Nutrition Therapy

The goal of nutrition intervention is to stop malnutrition, to promote weight gain by increasing energy intake and expanding dietary choices, and to restore normal perceptions of hunger and satiety. The first step is to assess nutritional status. Status is often so poor that medical nutrition therapy must start by simply increasing nutrient and energy intake to correct life-threatening malnutrition. An initial goal of nutritional therapy is a weight gain of 0.9 to 1.4 kilograms (2 to 3 lbs.) per week for inpatients and 0.23 to 0.45 kilograms (.5 to 1 lb.) per week in outpatient treatment. An initial target caloric intake is set at about 1,000 to 1,600 Calories per day (30–40 Calories per kilogram of body weight). As patients are able to consume this amount and weight increases, caloric intake is increased as needed to restore a healthy body weight. In some patients, force-feeding techniques such as tube or intravenous feedings may be necessary to provide adequate caloric intake. However, most medical professionals believe it is counterproductive to use force-feeding methods except in cases where these procedures are required to keep the patient alive. It is important to monitor patients during re-feeding. Their food and fluid intake should be monitored to assure that they are consuming what is offered. In addition, patients need to be checked for changes in vital signs and electrolyte levels, rapid weight gain, and gastrointestinal symptoms. Complications that may occur during re-feeding include low potassium and phosphorus levels, edema, fluid overload leading to rapid water-weight gain, congestive heart failure, constipation, and bloating.

Once the patient is medically stable, healthy target weights can be established. Physical activity should be adapted to the food intake and other energy expenditure of the patient. The individual and the family should be provided with information on energy needs and normal body weights, typical food intake patterns, and the risks of eating disorders. Programs should try to help patients deal with their concerns about weight gain and body image changes. Each individual patient must experiment with eating behaviors to develop healthy patterns that can be maintained over the long term. Self-monitoring techniques, such as food records, tracking laxative use and purging behaviors, and charting weight changes, can be helpful in learning normal eating behaviors.

Medications

Because starvation is known to worsen depression, the need for medication is best assessed after weight gain has occurred so the psychological effects of malnutrition are present and may be resolved. Antidepressants and tranquilizers are prescribed in some cases. They are used to prevent relapses in patients who have restored their weight to a healthy level or to treat some of the psychological problems associated with anorexia, such as depression, anxiety, and obsessive-compulsive problems. A medication called olanzapine (sold as Zyprexa®), which is typically used to treat schizophrenia, has recently been shown to be effective in reducing the obsessive thoughts about food and eating that affect most people with anorexia. However, because weight gain is one of the side effects of this drug, many people with anorexia refuse to take it. None of these medications is effective if used in isolation; the drugs must be combined with medical, behavioral, and psychological therapies.

Recovery

Recovery from anorexia is a lengthy process involving therapy and experimentation. Relapses to previous behaviors are common. Even after years of treatment, full recovery rates are only modest; after four years of follow-up, about two-thirds of patients continue to be preoccupied with weight and food. It is estimated that about 5% of anorexic patients die as a result of their eating disorder, primarily by heart attack or suicide. In general, those diagnosed during adolescence have a better prognosis than adults, and younger adolescents have a better outcome than older adolescents.[11]

CONNECTIONS

Anorexia is characterized by severe weight loss. It is a psychological disorder with a behavioral component and nutritional and medical consequences that is most common in women between 13 and 25 years of age. The psychological component involves a fear of gaining weight, disturbances in body image and perception of body size; anorexics use body weight and size as a means of self-evaluation. Perfectionism is so common in anorexics that it is considered a risk factor. Other psychological symptoms that are common in anorexia include depressed mood, irritability, social withdrawal, loss of sexual drive, and preoccupation with food. Physical characteristics include abnormalities in the menstrual cycle in women and sex hormone changes in men. Severe weight loss is the most visible sign of the disorder. The most prominent behavioral component is restriction of food intake; anorexics are preoccupied with food but eat very little. Hyperactivity and overactivity are also characteristic of anorexia. Many anorexics exercise excessively to burn calories—continuing to exercise beyond reasonable endurance. About half of anorexics use purging behaviors such as vomiting, laxatives, enemas, and diuretics to eliminate extra calories. Anorexia causes starvation; as the disease progresses, there is a depletion of body fat stores, muscle wasting, slowed growth, and a decrease in metabolic rate and body temperature. Almost every organ system is affected. In the final stages, life is threatened by electrolyte imbalances, dehydration, edema, cardiac abnormalities, and infection. The goal of treatment for patients with anorexia nervosa is to help resolve the psychological and behavioral problems while also providing for physical and nutritional rehabilitation. Psychological treatment cannot begin until the patient is medically stable and weight gain has begun.

8

Bulimia Nervosa

It is Friday night and I am alone in my room. I am bored and can't concentrate on my homework. I desperately want to eat. I feel myself losing control. Before I know it, I am at the convenience store. I go to three different stores so no one will know how much I am buying: two pints of ice cream, a supersized bag of chips, a one-pound package of cookies, a half dozen candy bars, and a quart of milk. Back in the privacy of my room, I start by eating the chips, then move through the cookies and the candy bars, washing them down with milk. I save the ice cream for last because eating ice cream makes it easier to vomit. Within an hour or two, all the food is gone. I am feeling gross and my stomach is bulging. Luckily, no one is around so the bathroom is empty—no one will hear me vomiting. When I finish, I rinse out my mouth because the stomach acid feels like it is burning my throat. I feel weak and guilty but also relieved. I straighten up my room, take a shower, and go to bed. Tomorrow, I will start a new diet. If I don't do something I will gain even more hideous fat than I already have.

This snapshot of bulimia nervosa shows us a person who is desperate to control her food intake but is overwhelmed by the urge to eat. When she can no longer resist the drive to eat, she binges by secretly eating large amounts of what she considers forbidden foods. Then, she engages in almost ritualistic behaviors to eliminate the excess calories she consumed. Repeated episodes of binging and purging begin to cause physical damage to her mouth and throat.

WHAT IS BULIMIA NERVOSA?

The name *bulimia* is taken from the Greek words *bous* ("ox") and *limos* ("hunger"), denoting hunger of such intensity that a person could eat an entire ox. Reports of gorging combined with vomiting exist in the early medical literature, but these were considered to be due primarily to stomach problems. The modern concept of bulimia nervosa as an eating disorder arose during the investigation of anorexia nervosa. Beginning in the early 1970s, a set of symptoms was identified and bulimia was distinguished from anorexia and obesity. Many different names were used for this disorder, including dysorexia, bulimarexia, thin-fat syndrome, binge/purge syndrome, and dietary chaos syndrome. The term *bulimia nervosa* was coined in 1979 by British psychiatrist Gerald Russell. He suggested that bulimia consisted of "powerful and intractable urges to overeat" in combination with "a morbid fear of becoming fat" and the avoidance of "the fattening effects of food by inducing vomiting or abusing purgatives or both."[22] Today, an estimated 1.1 to 4.2% of American females suffer from bulimia nervosa during their lifetime.[11]

CHARACTERISTICS OF BULIMIA

Bulimia nervosa most often occurs in women in their late teens and early twenties, but can develop at a younger age. It is rare in men. Bulimia is characterized by recurrent episodes of binge eating followed by purging behaviors such as vomiting, use of drugs, fasting, or excessive exercise to prevent weight gain. Unlike anorexia, it is not easy to identify someone with bulimia by looking at them. Most people with bulimia are close to or within the normal weight range for their age and height. They restrict calories between binges and use compensatory behaviors following the binge-eating episodes to prevent excessive weight gain.

As with anorexia, bulimia nervosa is a psychological disorder with a behavioral component as well as physical and nutritional consequences. The diagnosis of bulimia is based on the presence of recurrent episodes of binge eating; recurrent, inappropriate compensatory behaviors to prevent weight gain; and the use of body weight and shape as a means of self-evaluation. For a diagnosis of bulimia, binges must take place at least twice a week for three months. A binge is defined as eating, within a discrete period of time (such as two hours), an amount of food that is larger than most people would eat during a similar period of time under similar circumstances. One of the most important features distinguishing a binge from normal eating is the sense of a loss of control over eating (Table 8.1).

The behaviors used by bulimics to prevent weight gain are referred to as inappropriate compensatory behaviors. These include purging behaviors such as self-induced vomiting or misuse of laxatives, diuretics, enemas, or other medications; and nonpurging behaviors such as fasting or excessive exercise. There are two

---

FACT BOX 8.1

Intentional Vomiting Throughout History

Modern-day bulimics are not the only people who have been known to force themselves to throw up after a large meal. In fact, for centuries, people in some cultures have made themselves vomit not to prevent weight gain but to empty their stomachs so they could keep eating! Sources from ancient Rome mention the common practice of vomiting after a big feast. In his *Moral Epistles*, Roman philosopher Seneca wrote, "When we recline at a banquet, one [slave] wipes up the spittle; another, situated beneath [the table], collects the leavings of the drunks." And famous Roman orator Cicero mentioned in one of his writings that after a particular dinner, the emperor Julius Caesar said that he wanted to go and vomit. Clearly, people with bulimia nervosa are not alone in their practice of self-induced vomiting—although, traditionally, vomiting was done for very different reasons that were not at all related to weight loss.

Source: "Were There Really Vomitoriums in Ancient Rome?" *The Straight Dope*. Available online at http://www.straightdope.com/columns/021101.html.

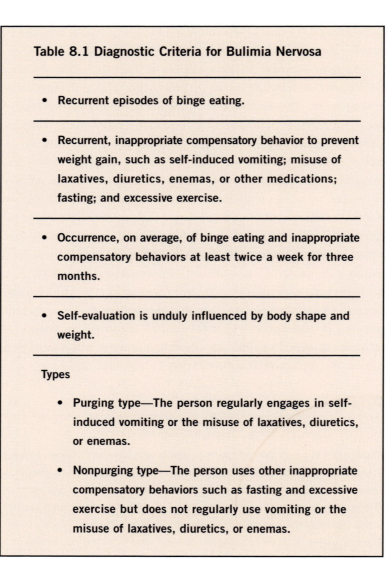

Table 8.1 Diagnostic Criteria for Bulimia Nervosa

- Recurrent episodes of binge eating.

- Recurrent, inappropriate compensatory behavior to prevent weight gain, such as self-induced vomiting; misuse of laxatives, diuretics, enemas, or other medications; fasting; and excessive exercise.

- Occurrence, on average, of binge eating and inappropriate compensatory behaviors at least twice a week for three months.

- Self-evaluation is unduly influenced by body shape and weight.

Types

- Purging type—The person regularly engages in self-induced vomiting or the misuse of laxatives, diuretics, or enemas.

- Nonpurging type—The person uses other inappropriate compensatory behaviors such as fasting and excessive exercise but does not regularly use vomiting or the misuse of laxatives, diuretics, or enemas.

categories of bulimia based on the types of compensatory behaviors used: purging type and nonpurging type. It is the purging type bulimics who regularly engage in self-induced vomiting and the misuse of enemas, laxatives, diuretics, or other medications. Nonpurging type bulimics are those who may fast or exercise excessively to prevent weight gain.

Psychological Disturbances

Bulimia nervosa shares with anorexia a preoccupation with body weight and shape. People with this disorder have an intense fear of becoming fat. They have a negative body image accompanied by a distorted perception of their body size. Their self-esteem is highly tied to their impressions of their body shape and weight. They are preoccupied with the fear that once they start eating, they will not be able to stop.

Many bulimics engage in continuous dieting, which leads to a preoccupation with food. These individuals spend a lot of time thinking about food, shopping for food, planning meals, and worrying about their bodies. When they do binge, the purge that follows serves to reduce tension but also makes them feel guilty.

People with bulimia blame all of their problems on their appearance; this allows them to avoid facing their real problems. They also think they are the only people in the world with this problem. As a result, they are often socially isolated. They may avoid situations that will expose them to food, such as going to parties or out to dinner, which further increases social isolation.

There is no single personality type that is characteristic of bulimia. Some bulimics are organized, successful perfectionists, while others lead disorderly, chaotic lives. Some are impulsive, sensitive, and have low self-esteem. Others are narcissistic with an inflated sense of self-importance and a need for attention and admiration. Many suffer from other disorders such as depression, psychosis, and substance abuse. The psychological profiles of purging and nonpurging type bulimics are different. Bulimics who purge tend to have greater body image disturbances, more anxiety concerning eating, and engage in more self-injurious behavior than do those who do not purge. They are also more likely to be depressed and to abuse alcohol.

Bulimics share many of the psychological characteristics and family situations common to anorexia but are better at hiding their disease behind a mask of independence and achievement. This is helped by the fact that they are typically older and are usually of normal weight.

Behavioral Component

The behavioral component that distinguishes bulimia from other eating disorders is the frequent binge/purge cycle (Figure 8.1). Bulimia typically begins with food restriction motivated by the desire to be thin. Overwhelming hunger may finally cause the dieting to be interrupted by a period of overeating. Eventually, a pattern develops involving semi-starvation interrupted by periods of gorging. These binges are followed by compensatory behaviors such as self-induced vomiting and laxative abuse.

Binges are often well planned. Food may be stored so it can be eaten at a time when no one will interrupt the binge. Binge foods are usually chosen because they are easy to swallow and regurgitate. They are typically fatty, sweet, high-calorie foods that bulimics would deny themselves at other times. Foods most commonly eaten during a binge include ice cream, bread, candy, doughnuts, soft drinks, sandwiches, cookies, popcorn, milk, cheese, and cereal. The food is eaten quickly, often being gulped and swallowed so fast that it can barely be tasted. After the first few minutes, the food consumption has nothing to do with hunger. During a food binge, a bulimic experiences a sense of lack of control. The amount of food a bulimic consumes during a binge varies, but is typically on the order of 3,400 Calories, compared with a normal teenager who may consume 2,000 to 3,000 Calories in an entire day. One study found that bulimics ate an average of about 7,000 Calories in a 24-hour period.[23] Binges usually last less than two hours and stop when the food runs out, or when pain, fatigue, or an interruption intervenes. The amount of food eaten during a binge may not always be enormous but it is still perceived by the bulimic individual as a binge episode.

Bulimic episodes are usually initiated by boredom, anxiety, or tension. They may be triggered by being reminded about food or exposed to food at a social gathering. Drinking alcohol or smoking marijuana can also trigger a binge, as can things such as anxiety about a date or fatigue from working hard. Before a binge, bulimics experience a powerful and irresistible urge to overeat, yet they rarely admit that hunger led to the binge, even if they have eaten very little for long periods prior to the binge.

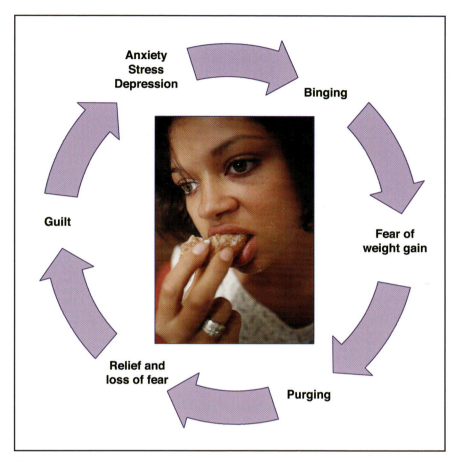

Figure 8.1 This cycle of binging and purging is typical of bulimia, although it may be a symptom of other eating disorders as well.

Usually, binges are kept secret and concealed from the patient's family for years. To hide the binge, evidence is cleaned up and the food eaten may be replaced so no one else in the house knows that it is gone. In some cases, however, the bulimic may leave clues such as empty food packages and evidence of vomiting, as if they wish to be discovered.

After these binge episodes, most bulimics use purging techniques such as vomiting or the abuse of laxatives or diuretics to eliminate the excess calories from their bodies. The most common behavior is self-induced vomiting. It is used at the end of a binge but also after normal eating to eliminate food before it is absorbed and the energy it provides can cause weight gain. At first, a physical maneuver such as sticking a finger down the throat is needed to induce vomiting but patients eventually learn to vomit at will. Vomiting may occur once or twice a day. It is accompanied by feelings of self-disgust but provides relief from the swollen stomach caused by binging and the fear of gaining weight. It can become habit forming and encourage further binging and, hence, additional vomiting. Laxatives are taken to induce diarrhea. Although the patients believe diarrhea prevents calories from being absorbed, in fact, nutrient absorption is almost complete before food enters the colon where laxatives work. Any weight loss associated with laxative abuse is due to dehydration. Diuretics also cause water loss, but via the kidney. They do not cause fat loss. A smaller number of bulimia sufferers resort to other methods of eliminating excess calories, such as extreme exercise or fasting. A few bulimics use a combination of purging and nonpurging methods.

People with bulimia usually binge and purge at least once a day, and, on average, about 12 times a week. After a binge, they

---

FACT BOX 8.2

How Many Calories Does Vomiting Eliminate?

The most common purging technique used by individuals with bulimia nervosa is self-induced vomiting. This is done to rid the body of the large number of calories consumed in a binge and therefore prevent weight gain. If it works, then why isn't the average bulimic thin? A study that measured the calories from a binge that remain in the stomach after vomiting found that, on average, 1,209 Calories were retained after a binge of 3,530 Calories. Interestingly, when the binge was smaller—only 1,549 Calories—the energy that remained in the stomach after vomiting was almost the same, at 1,128 Calories.

Source: Kaye, W.H., T.E. Weltzin, L.K. Hsu, C.W. McConaha, and B. Bolton. "Amount of calories retained after binge eating and vomiting." *American Journal of Psychiatry* 150 (1993): 969–971.

feel ashamed and disgusted with themselves for overeating, but feel relief from the purging. They are no longer uncomfortable from abdominal swelling and are gratified that they will not gain weight from the gorging. Binging and purging are then followed by intense feelings of guilt and shame. Despite this, bulimic episodes and subsequent purging have an anxiety-relieving effect.

Physical Effects of Bulimia

Bulimia is generally not fatal and those who do die generally have been diagnosed with anorexia as well at some time.[24] It is the purging portion of the binge/purge cycle that is most hazardous to the health in bulimia nervosa. The physical complications depend on the type of purging and the frequency with which it occurs. Purging by vomiting brings stomach acid into the esophagus and mouth, causing tooth decay and damaging the gastrointestinal tract. Gastrointestinal symptoms can include heartburn, sores in the mouth and on the lips, swollen jaws and salivary glands, irritation of the throat, esophageal inflammation, constipation, diarrhea, pancreatitis, and changes in stomach capacity and stomach emptying. Vomiting can also cause loss of water and electrolytes. This leads to dehydration, electrolyte imbalances, muscle cramps and weakness, dry skin, and menstrual irregularities. In addition, the force of vomiting can result in broken blood vessels in the face and eyes. Laxative and diuretic abuse can cause dehydration and electrolyte imbalances. This can lead to heart problems such as palpitations, irregular and missed heartbeats, low blood pressure, and heart failure. Rectal bleeding may occur from laxative overuse.

TREATING BULIMIA NERVOSA

The overall goal of therapy for people with bulimia nervosa is to separate eating from their emotions and from their perceptions of success, and to promote eating that corresponds to hunger and satiety. Treatment involves psychological treatment along with behavior modification and nutritional counseling. Medications are helpful in some cases.

Most patients with uncomplicated bulimia nervosa do not require hospitalization. However, hospitalization may be needed for patients who have not responded to outpatient treatment; in those with serious psychological symptoms, such as being suicidal or having other psychiatric disturbances; and in those with serious physical symptoms, such as changes in vital signs, electrolyte imbalances, uncontrolled vomiting, or vomiting blood.

Psychosocial Therapy

The goals of psychosocial counseling include reduction in or elimination of binge/purge episodes, improved attitude toward eating, minimization of food restriction, increased variety of food intake, and healthy exercise patterns. In addition, underlying issues such as identity formation, body image, sexual difficulties, and family dysfunction need to be addressed. Learning coping skills and problem-solving techniques can be helpful in reducing relapses.

In order to determine the best course of treatment, a comprehensive evaluation of the individual patient is needed to determine his or her cognitive and psychological development, family issues, and other psychopathology. Initial treatment most often uses behavior therapy to treat the binging and purging behaviors. Tools such as meal planning and self-monitoring may be helpful. Psychological issues related to body image and a sense of lack of control over eating must then be resolved. Treatment may involve individual or group therapy, depending on the needs of the patient. Patients with concurrent anorexia nervosa or severe personality disorders may benefit from extended psychotherapy.

Family therapy is often useful, especially when the patient is an adolescent still living with parents or an older patient with ongoing conflicted interactions with family members. Marriage counseling may be helpful for those with marital problems. Support groups such as Overeaters Anonymous may be beneficial in preventing relapse, but they are not recommended as the sole or initial therapy.

Medical Nutrition Therapy

Most patients with bulimia nervosa are of normal weight, so weight restoration is not a concern. Nutritional therapy must address the physiological imbalances caused by purging episodes. In addition, nutritional counseling can help reduce binging and purging behaviors. Bulimic patients require counseling to establish regular nonbinging meal patterns. Education about nutrient needs, food choices, the benefits of a varied diet, and normal eating habits is important in restoring healthy eating patterns. There is evidence that therapy programs that include dietary counseling and management are more successful than programs that do not address nutrition.

Medications

Medications are used to restore normal eating behavior and to treat underlying psychological symptoms. For most patients, antidepressant medications are effective as one component of initial treatment. They may be especially helpful for patients with significant symptoms of depression, anxiety, obsessions, or certain impulse disorder symptoms. Antidepressant medications can reduce the symptoms of binge eating and purging and may help prevent relapse. However, it has been shown that bulimia generally responds better to behavioral therapy than to pharmacotherapy.

Recovery

Little is known about the prognosis for untreated bulimia. For those who have undergone psychosocial therapy, short-term success is reported in 50 to 70% of patients. However, there is a relapse rate of about 30 to 50% in the first 6 months to 6 years after treatment. Long-term follow-up reveals that about 70% of patients recover, 10% stay fully symptomatic, and 20% have variable symptoms.[25] For some people, this disorder may remain a chronic problem throughout life.

CONNECTIONS

Bulimia nervosa is characterized by recurrent episodes of binge eating followed by purging with abnormal compensatory behaviors such as vomiting, use of drugs, fasting, or excessive exercise to prevent weight gain. It is most common in women in their late teens and early twenties. The psychological component of bulimia nervosa includes a preoccupation with body weight and shape, an intense fear of becoming fat, and a negative body image accompanied by a distorted perception of body size. The frequent binge/purge cycle distinguishes bulimia from other eating disorders. Bulimic episodes occur in secret, usually brought on by boredom, anxiety, or tension. An average binge involves out-of-control eating of foods that the individuals would deny themselves at other times; it usually includes about 3,400 Calories eaten in less than 2 hours. After binging, bulimics typically purge by vomiting to eliminate calories. The purging provides a feeling of relief but the cycle is then followed by intense feelings of guilt and shame. Purging is hazardous to the health because vomiting brings stomach acid into the esophagus and mouth, causing gastrointestinal problems and tooth decay. Vomiting, as well as abuse of laxatives and diuretics, cause dehydration and electrolyte imbalances. Treatment of bulimia involves psychological treatment along with behavior modification and nutritional counseling in order to stop the binge/purge cycle, to separate eating from perceptions of success, and to promote eating in response to hunger and satiety.

9

Binge Eating and Other Eating Disorders

A third class of eating disorders, termed "eating disorders not otherwise specified," or EDNOS, includes conditions that meet the definition of an eating disorder but not the criteria for anorexia or bulimia (Table 9.1). Over 50% of all patients who seek treatment for an eating disorder do not fit the criteria for a diagnosis of either anorexia nervosa or bulimia nervosa and are therefore categorized as having an EDNOS.[11] These eating disorders are particularly common among adolescents. Most of these patients have subclinical cases of either anorexia or bulimia. This means that they meet some but not all of the criteria needed for diagnosis of one of these disorders. For example, a person may be restricting food intake and has stopped menstruating but has not lost enough weight to meet the criteria for anorexia of being 15% below healthy body weight. Alternatively, an individual who is binging and then purging with laxatives but only engaging in these behaviors a few times a month does not meet the criteria for bulimia. The eating disorders that fall within the EDNOS category

Table 9.1 Diagnostic Criteria for Eating Disorders Not Otherwise Specified (EDNOS)

- Criteria for anorexia nervosa are met, but the individual menstruates regularly.

- Criteria for anorexia nervosa are met except that, despite substantial weight loss, the individual's current weight is in the normal range.

- Criteria for bulimia nervosa are met except binges occur at a frequency of less than twice a week and for a duration of less than three months.

- Inappropriate compensatory behavior after eating small amounts of food in individuals of normal body weight.

- Regularly chewing and spitting out large amounts of food without swallowing.

- Binge-eating disorder: Recurrent episodes of binge eating in the absence of the regular use of the inappropriate compensatory behaviors characteristic of bulimia.

include binge-eating disorder and other eating disorders that have characteristics that distinguish them from anorexia and bulimia. Eating disorders of all kinds also appear in subpopulations, such as children, men, pregnant women, individuals with diabetes, and athletes. In these groups the frequency, causes, symptoms, and consequences of the eating disorder may vary from what is typical.

BINGE-EATING DISORDER

My weight is up to 160 pounds and I am only 5 feet, 4 inches tall. I am gross and disgusting and I know I eat too much. I just can't control my eating like other girls. When I am bored or depressed, the only relief I get is from a box of cookies and a carton of ice cream. After eating all this food, I feel even worse. I am always on a diet but I get so tired of giving up foods I like that I lose control and pig out. I know my eating and my weight are not healthy but I just can't seem to stop.

Binge-eating disorder (BED) is probably the most common eating disorder. According to the National Institutes of Health, it affects up to 4 million Americans. Individuals with this disorder typically binge but do not use compensatory methods to rid themselves of the excess calories; therefore, they are typically overweight. Binge-eating disorder affects 2 to 3% of the total American adult population and about 8% of the obese population. Unlike anorexia and bulimia, binge-eating disorder is not uncommon in men; it occurs in a female-to-male ratio of about 1.5 to 1. Compared to anorexia or bulimia, BED occurs in an older population. It is most common in people between 30 and 50 years of age.

Characteristics of Binge-Eating Disorder

Individuals who suffer from binge-eating disorder engage in recurrent episodes of binge eating but do not regularly use purging behaviors such as vomiting, fasting, or excessive exercise (Figure 9.1). People with this disorder are likely to have above-normal body weights; they are often identified when they seek treatment for obesity rather than for their binge-eating behavior.[26] About one-quarter to one-third of people who attend weight loss clinics meet the criteria for binge-eating disorder.

In order to be diagnosed with binge-eating disorder, a person must experience recurrent episodes of binge eating. The binge eating must occur, on average, at least 2 days a week for 6 months. The binge eating must also be associated with three or more factors, including 1) eating much more rapidly than normal, 2) eating until

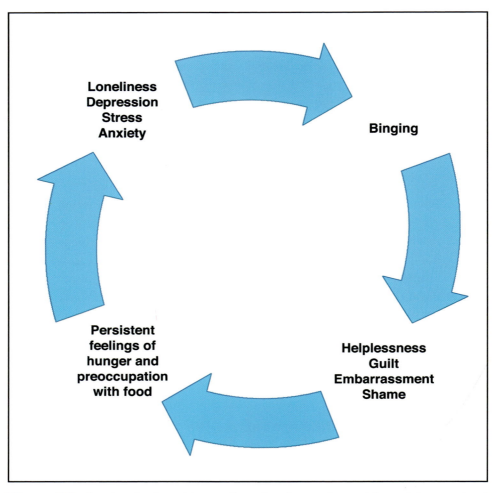

Figure 9.1 People who have binge-eating disorder are trapped in a vicious cycle of binging that typically leads to weight gain.

feeling uncomfortably full, 3) eating large amounts of food when not feeling physically hungry, 4) eating alone because of embarrassment about how much one is eating, or 5) feeling disgusted with oneself, depressed, or very guilty about eating. As with bulimia, the binge eating causes psychological distress and is accompanied by a sense of lack of control, a feeling that you cannot stop eating or control what or how much you eat. Unlike bulimics, binge eaters do not regularly use inappropriate compensatory behaviors such as purging, fasting, or excessive exercise. Therefore, many people with binge-eating disorder are overweight for their age and height. Feelings of self-disgust and shame that go along with this illness can lead to binging again, creating a cycle of binge eating.

Individuals with binge-eating disorder have abnormal attitudes toward body weight and shape. They are dissatisfied with their body image to an extent similar to what is seen with bulimia and more severe than is seen with overweight people who do not binge eat. They may also suffer from low self-esteem and depression. These individuals usually hide their eating and feel ashamed after a binge. They tend to have trouble functioning in social situations.

Treatment of BED

A program that includes a very low-calorie diet along with behavioral therapy has been shown to be effective in the treatment of binge-eating disorder. This method of treatment usually leads to significant weight loss and a reduction in binging behavior. However, after the initial weight loss, the patient generally gains back some of the weight in the year following treatment. Chronic dieting has been shown to lead to compensatory overeating as well as depression, anxiety, and irritability. To prevent these problems, newer treatment methods focus on self-acceptance, improved body image, a healthier diet, and increased exercise rather than weight-loss dieting. When compared to the traditional diet approaches, these non-diet programs have had similar results in terms of long-term weight reduction and are better at eliminating depression, anxiety, and body dissatisfaction. Antidepressants have also been used to treat binge-eating disorder. They are effective in some cases, but studies have also shown high rates of response with placebos.[11]

NIGHT-EATING SYNDROME

Night-eating syndrome is another eating disorder that is linked to obesity. It was first described in 1955 as a disorder that involves a lack of hunger in the morning followed by insomnia and excessive eating at night. It occurs more often in obese individuals and during periods in life when stress is great. It is sometimes alleviated by the elimination of the stress. The prevalence of night-eating syndrome in the general population is estimated to be about 1.5% but the frequency increases as body weight increases. The incidence rises to about 10% among people who enroll in obesity clinics and is as high as 25% in those undergoing obesity surgery. The pattern of caloric intake in people with night-eating syndrome is striking. A study that compared night eaters to obese individuals who are not night eaters (control subjects) found that by 6:00 P.M., the obese control subjects had consumed 74% of their energy for the day. Night eaters had consumed only 37%. The obese control subjects slowed their food intake in the evening, while the night eaters continued at a rapid rate until after midnight. From 8:00 P.M. to 6:00 A.M., night eaters consumed 56% of their energy, compared to 15% for obese controls.[27]

Night-eating syndrome appears to be not only an eating disorder, but also a sleep disorder and a mood disorder. Night eaters have difficulty falling asleep and staying asleep. They wake up more than 3 times per night. About half of the times they wake up, they eat. Each of these snacks contains about 270 Calories and is high in

---

FACT BOX 9.1

Fat Discrimination

Obese people in our society face prejudice because of their size. They are discriminated against at work, in school, in access to public accommodations, and in receiving adequate medical care. They are the victims of jokes; people tend to blame them for their condition. It is hard for them to succeed in business and in their personal lives. To try to combat this unfair discrimination, organizations such as the National Association to Advance Fat Acceptance have been founded. These groups work to end size discrimination, to educate the public, and to help overweight people demand their civil rights.

carbohydrates (70%) and relatively low in protein.[27] This preference for high carbohydrates may be related to the effect of carbohydrates on the neurotransmitter serotonin, which has sleep-promoting properties. High-carbohydrate foods make more of the amino acid tryptophan available to the brain; tryptophan can be converted to serotonin. Night eaters also had significant differences from other people in their levels of certain hormones, including melatonin, leptin, and cortisol. Abnormalities in melatonin may play a part in the sleep and mood disturbances. Leptin is a hormone that tends to rise at night. This rise suppresses appetite. In night eaters, leptin levels do not rise, and this may contribute to the hunger impulses, which may further disturb sleep. High levels of cortisol indicate that a person is under stress.

EATING DISORDERS IN CHILDHOOD

Although eating disorders occur most often in people in their teens and twenties, these disorders do happen occasionally in younger patients. The term *childhood-onset eating disorders* refers to eating disorders in individuals under the age of 13. The eating disorders seen in this age group include anorexia nervosa, bulimia (although it is rare among younger people), food-avoidance emotional disorder, selective eating, and pervasive refusal syndrome.

Anorexia

The incidence of anorexia in children is lower than it is in late adolescence and early adulthood, but it appears to be increasing, and the proportion of boys who have it is greater than the proportion of anorexic men in older age groups.

FACT BOX 9.2

Children Are Not Immune to Eating Disorders

- 42% of girls in 1st through 3rd grades want to be thinner.
- 81% of 10-year-olds are afraid of being fat.
- 50% of 9-year-old girls have dieted to lose weight.

Diagnosing anorexia in girls under 14 is more challenging than in older girls because some of the diagnostic criteria are difficult to interpret. Many girls may not have started menstruating, so doctors cannot take the absence of menstrual periods into account. It is also hard to calculate expected weight accurately because growth may have slowed. Despite these problems, there is little doubt that childhood-onset anorexia does occur and is a serious illness.

Children with anorexia have symptoms similar to those of older subjects. These include weight loss, food avoidance, preoccupation with food and calories, fear of fatness, excessive exercise, self-induced vomiting, and laxative abuse. Other physical changes that may accompany the weight loss include growth of lanugo hair, low blood pressure, slow heart rate, poor peripheral circulation, cold arms and legs, and slowed or stunted growth. Bone density may be reduced and bone age delayed. Vitamin and mineral deficiencies are common.

Children with anorexia have similar personality traits to older people with the disorder. They are described as pleasant children who are perfectionists, conscientious, and hardworking. The children may hide the fact that they are not eating by secretly disposing of food or eating separately from the family. Girls tend to say they are dieting to be thin to look attractive, whereas boys more commonly claim they are dieting to improve their health and fitness. Exercise is a common way to control weight in this age group. It is socially acceptable. If parents restrict activities like swimming and running, anorexic children may replace them with other activities, such as stair climbing and push-ups—as many as several hundred a day. Self-induced vomiting and laxative abuse are less common among this age group.

The prognosis for children with anorexia is poor, with only between half and two-thirds making full recoveries. Complications that may persist include amenorrhea, delayed growth, impaired fertility, and osteoporosis.

Food-Avoidance Emotional Disorder

Food-avoidance emotional disorder is an eating disorder that only occurs in childhood. It is similar to anorexia nervosa in that the sufferer avoids eating. The distorted body image and the fear of gaining weight characteristic of anorexia are absent, however. Weight loss and the physical symptoms that go along with it, though, are as severe as or even worse than that seen with anorexia.

Selective Eating

This disorder is an extension of normal food finickiness that often occurs in preschool children. Children with this condition will usually eat only about 4 or 5 foods willingly. These foods are usually high in carbohydrates. Energy intake does not seem to be low, as indicated by the fact that the children do not lose weight or stop growing. The children are not overly concerned with their weight, shape, or body size. There seem to be few complications other than social restrictions. Selective eating is more common in boys than in girls.

Pervasive Refusal Syndrome

This is a life-threatening condition seen in children. It is characterized by a refusal not only to eat but also to drink, talk, walk, or care for oneself in any way. This disorder is often the result of some type of trauma, such as sexual abuse or violence.

EATING DISORDERS IN MEN

The occurrence of eating disorders in men is not a new phenomenon. It has been reported since 1689. The incidence is much lower than in women, however, with only about 10 to 20% of cases of anorexia occurring in men. Bulimia is very uncommon in men.

It is possible that men have a lower incidence of eating disorders because they face less social pressure to be thin. Beginning in elementary school, boys are less likely than girls to think they need to diet, even though they may be equally dissatisfied with their bodies. Some boys want to lose weight and an equal number want to be bigger; all want to be more muscular. Men are not as affected by the social pressure to be thin and to diet. If an adult man describes himself as overweight, he is typically 15% heavier (compared with his ideal body weight) than an adult woman who describes herself as overweight. Women feel thin when they are at about 90% of their ideal body weight, whereas men describe themselves as feeling thin when they are as heavy as 105% of their ideal. The desire to lose weight is greatest in certain subgroups of men, including those who wrestle, homosexuals, and those who are obese.

Even though men may not be under as much pressure as women to be thin, they are still influenced by the social ideal for a male body—a V-shaped upper body that is muscular, moderate in weight, and low in body fat. This ideal is portrayed in action toys, superhero cartoons, and media images. To look like the typical superhero, the average healthy male would need to be 20 inches taller, and make his chest 11 inches larger and his neck 7.9 inches larger.[28] Advertisements directed at men today show more and more exposed skin, with a focus on well-defined abdominal and chest muscles (Figure 9.2).

The diagnostic criteria for men with eating disorders is similar to those for women. Both have an abnormality in reproductive hormones; however, rather than the abrupt cessation of menstruation seen in women, in men there is a gradual drop in testosterone levels. This causes a loss of sexual desire. Men with eating disorders have psychiatric conditions that are similar to those that affect women, including mood and personality problems. Both men and women lose bone but males are more severely affected by disorders related to bone loss and tend to have lower bone mineral density than their female counterparts.

Treatment is similar for men and women, but some modifications are needed when treating men. Males typically have higher energy needs than females, so caloric intakes may need to be significantly higher than intakes for females. Group therapy may be more effective if the group includes only males rather than males and females together. The outcome of treatment is similar in men and women.

EATING DISORDERS AND PREGNANCY

Eating disorders are common in women in their twenties. Since this is an age when many people choose to start a family, it is not

Figure 9.2 The standards for the ideal male body are as difficult for most men to achieve as the thin athletic ideal is for women. This leads many men to suffer low self-esteem or to exercise obsessively.

unusual to find women with eating disorders who are pregnant. Pregnancy is a time when nutritional health is particularly important. A woman must meet her own nutritional needs as well as the additional needs of supporting the growth and development of the baby.

Women with eating disorders may have difficulty conceiving and carrying a baby to term. In anorexia, the absence of a menstrual cycle will prevent pregnancy from occurring, but women with less severe eating disorders or with bulimia may still be able to conceive. When she becomes pregnant, a woman with an eating disorder may become depressed and frantic about the accompanying weight gain. She may feel so out of control that she hurts herself or the baby. In contrast, some women welcome pregnancy as a break from concerns about weight. Having the baby is important enough for them to put aside their fear of becoming fat.

Pregnant women with eating disorders have a higher rate of miscarriages, premature birth, and babies who are small at birth. Pregnant women who have eating disorders are at increased risk of caesarean delivery and postpartum depression. Pregnancy can also worsen other medical problems related to the eating disorder, such as liver, heart, and kidney damage.

What and how much a woman eats during pregnancy influences the baby after birth. Babies born to women with eating disorders are more likely to be smaller, weaker, and slower growing. They are also more likely to be slow to develop. They may lag behind intellectually and emotionally and remain dependent. They may also have difficulty developing social skills and relationships with other people. Infants of undernourished mothers have a higher rate of heart disease and diabetes when they get older than babies of well-nourished mothers. For some of these long-term problems, it is difficult to determine whether they are the result of the eating disorder during pregnancy or due to being raised by a parent with emotional problems (Figure 9.3).

EATING DISORDERS AND DIABETES

Diabetes is a disease characterized by a chronic elevation in blood glucose level that results when the body does not effectively produce or use the hormone insulin, which is responsible for allowing glucose to enter body cells. This disease is treated through a combination of diet, exercise, and, in some cases, medication. The goal of treatment is to keep blood glucose levels

Figure 9.3 A pregnant woman with an eating disorder puts herself and her unborn child at risk.

within the normal range. People with diabetes must pay close attention to their body state and weight as well as to the type and amount of food they eat and the timing and content of meals. For a diabetic, some foods are considered safe and good, whereas others are dangerous and bad. Control is therefore a central issue in diabetes, as it is in eating disorders. A person with diabetes may feel guilty or out of control if his or her blood sugar is too high. Anorexics feel the same way if their weight increases. People with diabetes may become obsessed with strategies to control blood sugar just as people with eating disorders become consumed with ways to control weight. Both are preoccupied with weight, food, and diet. Because this is expected in diabetes, people with this disease can use their diabetes to hide anorexia or bulimia. They are supposed to watch what they eat and they can blame the diabetes for any unusual weight loss.

Diabetes is not a cause of eating disorders, but it does set the stage for them both physically and emotionally and can be used to hide them. Some scientists believe that eating disorders are more common among diabetics than in the general population. Those who take insulin to control their diabetes are at particular risk because they can misuse it to control their weight. If they cut back on the amount of insulin they take, the sugar in their blood cannot enter cells and is excreted in the urine. This will cause weight loss, but at a very high cost. The long-term complications of having high levels of blood glucose include cardiovascular disease, blindness, kidney disease, nerve damage, impaired circulation, and infections that can lead to limb amputations. People with diabetes and eating disorders believe that being fat is far worse than these complications. They may argue that these problems may happen in the future, but being fat could happen today. Once diabetics start to control their weight by withholding insulin, they are reluctant to stop and may also begin to use other behaviors to control weight. Sometimes, the weight loss seems to improve the diabetes, at least temporarily, by reducing or eliminating the need for insulin. If the weight loss continues, however, it eventually leads to organ failure and death.

EATING DISORDERS IN ATHLETES

The relationship between body weight and performance in certain sports puts many athletes at risk for eating disorders. One type of eating disorder that may occur among athletes is anorexia nervosa. The regimented schedule of athletes makes it easy for them to use training diets and schedules, travel, or competition as an excuse not to eat normally and as a way to hide the eating disorder. Athletes who are anorexic restrict food intake and use behaviors such as vomiting after eating, abuse of laxatives, and excessive exercise to eliminate or use up calories to maintain a very low weight. Over time, the continued starvation characteristic of anorexia leads to serious health problems as well as a decline in athletic performance. Starvation can lead to abnormal heart rhythms, low blood pressure, and atrophy of the heart muscle. The lack of food means that there is not adequate energy and nutrients to support activity and growth. Sleep disorders are also common in anorexia.

The eating disorder bulimia nervosa is more common in athletes than is anorexia. Bulimia may begin because an athlete is unable to stick to a restrictive diet or because the hunger that results from a very low-calorie diet leads to binging. Those with bulimia are usually of normal or higher than normal body weight. Most of the health complications associated with bulimia are the result of the binge/purge cycle.

FACT BOX 9.3

The Risk of Eating Disorders Is Greater in Some Sports

Ninety-three percent of eating disorders in athletes involve women's sports. Most female athletes with eating disorders take part in cross country, gymnastics, swimming, or track and field events. The male sports with the highest number of participants with eating disorders are wrestling and cross country.[a]

[a] ANRED (Anorexia Nervosa and Related Eating Disorders, Inc.). "Athletes with eating disorders: An overview." Available online at *http://www.anred.com/ath_intro.html*.

Compulsive exercise is a type of eating disorder that is a particular problem in athletes. It has less to do with food but is considered an eating disorder because athletes exercise compulsively to burn off calories to control weight. Compulsive exercisers use extreme training as a means of purging calories. This behavior is easy to justify because it is a common belief that serious athletes can never work too hard or too long, and pain is accepted as an indicator of achievement. Compulsive exercisers will force themselves to exercise even when they don't feel well and may miss social events in order to fulfill their exercise quota. They often calculate exercise goals based on how much they eat. They believe that any break in the training schedule will cause them to gain weight and their athletic performance will suffer. Compulsive exercise can lead to more serious eating disorders such as anorexia and bulimia and can cause severe health problems, including kidney failure, heart attack, and death.

CONNECTIONS

Eating disorders not otherwise specified (EDNOS) are a group of conditions that do not meet the diagnostic criteria for anorexia or bulimia. Binge-eating disorder, which is the most common eating disorder, falls into this category. It is characterized by episodes of binge eating in the absence of purging or other inappropriate compensatory behaviors. Individuals with binge-eating disorder tend to be overweight and often seek treatment for their weight rather than their binge eating. Treatment focuses on self-acceptance, improved body image, a nutritious diet, and increased exercise rather than weight loss. Night-eating syndrome is a disorder that involves a lack of hunger in the morning, followed by insomnia and excessive eating at night. A number of eating disorders, including anorexia, food-avoidance emotional disorder, selective eating, and pervasive refusal syndrome are seen in children. Eating disorders occur in men but at a lower rate than in women, possibly because men are not as severely affected by societal messages to be thin. Eating disorders during pregnancy can put the mother at risk, as well as cause short-term and long-term problems for the baby. People with diabetes have control issues similar to those seen with eating disorders. The preoccupation with food, diet, and weight, as well as the need for self-monitoring that are a part of life for diabetics, put them at risk. It is particularly dangerous if they withhold insulin as a way to lose weight. Athletes with eating disorders compromise their health and performance.

10

Staying Healthy

Being excessively concerned about your weight can increase your risk of developing an eating disorder. That is not to say you should ignore your body weight. Maintaining a healthy body image and managing your weight at a realistic level are both important to your physical and mental health and to preventing eating disorders. To accomplish this, you need to eat a healthy diet and get enough exercise.

WHAT SHOULD YOU WEIGH?

Having a healthy body weight improves your chances of living a long and healthy life. Carrying excess body fat increases your risk of heart disease, diabetes, stroke, gallbladder disease, sleep disorders, respiratory problems, and some types of cancer. Keeping your weight at a healthy level reduces the risk of these diseases.

Your healthy weight depends on your age, gender, and genetic background, as well as your lifestyle. As you grow, your body changes in size and composition. You get taller and heavier as you grow from a child to a teen and then to an adult. If you are female, the amount of body fat you have will increase as you pass through puberty. If you are male, you will gain proportionately more muscle mass. Your body's final size, weight, and composition depend on your genes and lifestyle. If your parents are both broad-shouldered and 6 feet tall, it is unlikely that you will be petite. Likewise, if your mother has a pear-shaped body, carrying extra weight in her hips and thighs, it is likely that you will develop that shape, too. But, if you exercise and eat right, whatever shape you inherit will be lean and fit.

What Is Your Healthy Body Weight?

The first step in determining the body weight that is healthy for you is to calculate your BMI. For adults, this value can be compared to the values in Figure 6.1 to see if weight is in the healthy range. For children and teens, this value can be plotted on a growth chart to see where it falls in comparison to others of the same age and gender (see Appendix C). In general, a healthy BMI is between the 5th and the 85th percentiles; a BMI that is between the 85th and 95th percentiles is considered at risk for overweight, and a BMI greater than the 95th percentile is considered overweight (Figure 10.1). When evaluating body weight, it is important to consider factors other than BMI. For example, sometimes in children and teens, body weight may increase just before a growth spurt, so BMI may be high for a period of a few months and then, once the growth occurs, BMI will go back to the healthy range. Body composition is also important. For instance, if you are an athlete such as a football player or weight lifter with a large proportion of muscle, then you may be at a healthy weight despite the fact that your BMI is high.

Balancing What You Eat With What You Use

Diet and exercise are both essential for maintaining a healthy weight. If you are at a healthy weight, you can stay there by balancing the calories you consume in your diet with the energy you expend to stay alive, grow, and be active. If you take in more calories than you

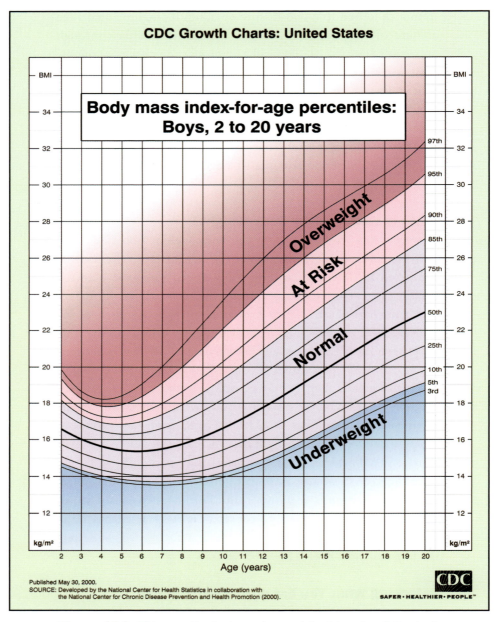

Figure 10.1 This growth chart can be used to determine if the body mass index of a boy between the ages of 2 and 20 is in the healthy range. A similar chart for girls ages 2 to 20 can be found in Appendix C.

need to stay healthy and grow, you will store the extra energy, mostly as body fat. If you eat fewer calories than you expend, you will use stored body fat and lose weight. In children and teens, a prolonged deficit in energy will stop growth in height. Choosing a diet that is rich in whole grains and fruits and vegetables and moderate in fat can make balancing intake with expenditure easier. Regular exercise helps because it increases the amount of energy you use and thereby allows you to eat more food without gaining weight. For example, an active 20-year-old woman needs to take in about 500 Calories more per day to maintain weight than a sedentary woman of the same age, height, and weight.

WHAT IS A HEALTHY DIET?

A healthy diet is one that provides the right number of calories to keep your weight in the appropriate range; the proper balance of carbohydrates, protein, and fat choices; plenty of water; and sufficient but not excessive amounts of essential vitamins and minerals. Generally, recommendations from the Food Guide Pyramid and the Dietary Guidelines suggest a diet that is rich in whole grains, fruits,

---

FACT BOX 10.1

Is Your Body Mass Index in the Healthy Range?

To find out if your body weight is in the healthy range, you need to do a calculation to determine your body mass index (BMI):

1) Measure your weight in pounds and your height in inches.

2) Divide your weight by your height, then divide the answer by your height again.

3) Multiply the answer by 703.

4) If you are 20 years old or younger, use Appendix C to see whether your BMI is in the healthy range for someone your age.

5) If you are over 20 years of age and your answer falls between 18.5 and 24.9, your BMI is within the healthy range.

and vegetables. This dietary pattern is high in essential nutrients and fiber, moderate in fat and sodium, and low in saturated fat, cholesterol, and added sugars. When you eat these foods, you are also getting other health-promoting substances such as **phytochemicals**. Foods high in phytochemicals often have health benefits beyond those provided by the nutrients they contain. Choosing this diet doesn't mean giving up your favorite foods. But it does mean balancing treats with more nutrient-dense choices at other times. For example, foods that are low in **nutrient density**, such as baked goods, snack foods, and sodas, should be balanced with nutrient-dense choices such as salads, fresh fruit, and large vegetable servings. If your favorite meal is a burger, fries, and a milkshake, enjoy it, but balance it with a salad, brown rice, and baked chicken at the next meal.

How Much Carbohydrate, Fat, and Protein?

There is no set proportion of carbohydrate, fat, and protein that defines a healthy diet, but the types of carbohydrates, fats, and proteins chosen are important. Carbohydrates come from grains, fruits, vegetables, and dairy products as well as from added sugars in baked goods and sweetened beverages like soda. The key to choosing a healthy mix of carbohydrates is to eat carbohydrate sources that are less refined. Refining tends to add sugar, salt, and fat, and take out fiber. Stick with less refined foods by choosing whole-wheat bread and oatmeal from the bottom level of the Food Guide Pyramid rather than white bread and sugar puffs. Choose fresh blueberries rather than a blueberry pie from the fruit group and fresh tomatoes rather than ketchup from the vegetable group.

When it comes to fat choices, monounsaturated and polyun-saturated fats are better for your health than saturated fat, *trans* fat, and cholesterol. You can get the right mix of fats by choosing mostly vegetable fats; olive oil, canola oil, and peanut oil are high in monounsaturated fat; other vegetable oils are high in polyunsaturated fats. Saturated fat and cholesterol are found mainly in animal products such as beef and whole milk, so a diet that includes few animal products will be low in these fats. *Trans* fat is found in products containing hydrogenated oils, such as solid margarines and shortening. To lower *trans* fat intake, you need to limit these added fats as well as baked goods and other foods that contain them. Soft or liquid margarines and cooking oils are lower in *trans* fats than stick margarine is. Fruits, vegetables, and whole grains are naturally cholesterol-free and are low in saturated and *trans* fat as long as these fats are not added to them during preparation.

FACT BOX 10.2

Where's the Added Sugar?

How much sugar is in a carton of yogurt? It doesn't take a detective to find the answer. The number of grams of sugars in a serving is listed on the Nutrition Facts label; a cup of strawberry yogurt has 37 grams. However, this number doesn't tell you whether the sugar came from the milk and strawberries used to make the yogurt, or if it was added to sweeten the final product. It turns out that there is no way to know for sure from the Nutrition Facts label how much of the total is added sugars. Sometimes, a label will say "no added sugar" or "without added sugar"—this tells you that no sugars were added in processing. The ingredient list also gives you some information about the sweeteners added to a food. Only added sugars are listed here. The weights of ingredients are not given, but ingredients are listed in order of prominence by weight, so the closer an ingredient is to the top of the list, the more of it there is in the food. In the strawberry yogurt, sugar is the second ingredient. This means that sucrose, the only sugar that can be called "sugar" in the ingredients list, is present in the second greatest amount by weight of all the ingredients used in making the yogurt. There may also be other sugars used, but to find them, you need to increase your sugar vocabulary. High-fructose corn syrups, invert sugar, dextrose, lactose, and honey are just a few types of sugars. In the case of the strawberry yogurt, sugar is the second ingredient and high-fructose corn syrup is the fourth ingredient. The amount of added sugar is the sum of these two sources of sugar. If you are looking for a product without added sugars, always check the ingredients list to be sure you know what you are getting.

Most Americans eat plenty of protein but which proteins you pick affects the types of fat and the amount of fiber in your diet. Animal sources of protein, such as beef and cheese, contain no fiber and are often high in saturated fat and cholesterol. You can cut down on the saturated fat in meats by trimming off the fat and cooking it in ways that don't add fat. For instance, frying food adds fat whereas barbecuing allows the fat to drip into the fire instead of into you. Choosing whole grains and legumes to provide some of your protein helps keep your diet low in saturated fat and cholesterol, and high in fiber.

Getting Your Vitamins and Minerals

Most foods naturally contain some vitamins and minerals, so unrefined foods are good sources. Cooking, storage, and processing can cause the loss of some of these from foods, but processing can also add vitamins and minerals to foods. The addition of nutrients to foods is called **fortification**. Some food fortification is mandatory. For example, in the United States, refined grains products must be fortified with the vitamins thiamin, niacin, riboflavin, and folic acid and the mineral iron. Fortification is also a marketing tool used by food manufacturers to make products more appealing to customers. For example, to increase sales, breakfast cereals are often fortified with so many vitamins that they resemble a multivitamin supplement. Foods fortified with nutrients such as calcium and iron, which are low in the American diet, can make it easier for many people to meet their needs. However, some foods are fortified with large amounts, so when you choose fortified foods, you need to make sure your intake does not exceed the UL or tolerable upper intake levels, for any nutrient.

Dietary supplements are another source of vitamins and minerals in the American diet. Though most people can meet their needs by consuming a varied, balanced diet, individuals who have increased needs, such as pregnant women and children, those whose intake is limited by dietary restrictions, and those whose absorption or utilization is limited by disease may need supplements to meet their needs. Consumers need to be aware, however, that supplements pose a toxicity risk. Although it is difficult to consume a toxic amount of a vitamin by eating foods, it is easy to get a large dose in a supplement. Many supplements on the market today also contain substances that are not nutrients, such as herbs. Some of these are safe, but others may have side effects that outweigh any benefits they provide. Because the manufacture of dietary supplements is not strictly regulated and supplements may not be stringently tested for safety before they are marketed, supplements that are dangerous may be on the market for years before enough evidence has accumulated to remove them. If you take supplements, do so with caution.

Meals and Snacks: How Often Should You Eat?

There is no one ideal number of meals and snacks you should eat each day. Both meals and snacks are part of a healthy diet. Snacks are especially important for young children and growing teens because these individuals may not be able to consume enough energy during meals to meet needs. If snacks are chosen wisely, they are an important source of essential nutrients as well as calories.

Skipping meals is not recommended. The body burns calories all day long and needs to replace used fuels. This is why breakfast is so important. When you wake up, you typically have not eaten for 12 or more hours. You need food to maintain blood glucose and to replenish liver glycogen stores. Students who eat breakfast have been shown to do better in school than those who skip breakfast. In addition, people who eat breakfast are less likely to overeat later in

---

FACT BOX 10.3

Who Checks Supplements for Safety?

According to the Dietary Supplement Health and Education Act of 1994, supplement manufacturers are responsible for ensuring that their products are safe. The Food and Drug Administration (FDA) only gets involved after the product is already on the market. The FDA collects information about suspected problems with dietary supplements and has the authority to remove products from the market if it can prove that the product carries significant health risks.

the day. Therefore, people who are trying to lose weight or maintain a healthy weight should eat breakfast.

Mix It Up! Variety Is Important

Even if your choices are healthy, variety is important. Foods provide unlimited combinations of nutrients. So, even if you are choosing something as healthy as broccoli for dinner, it is important to choose different vegetables on other days or for other meals. Each food provides a unique mix of vitamins, minerals, and phytochemicals. For example, strawberries are a fruit that provides vitamin C but little vitamin A, whereas apricots provide a source of vitamin A, but less vitamin C. If you choose only strawberries, you will get plenty of vitamin C but may be lacking in vitamin A.

How Much Should You Eat?

How much you need to eat depends on how many calories your body uses. Your body needs energy to stay alive and grow, to keep your heart beating, your kidneys working, and your body warm. It needs energy to digest the food you eat and to process the nutrients it contains. It also needs energy to fuel activity. Your caloric needs can be estimated by calculating your estimated energy requirement (EER) using an equation that takes into account your age, gender, height, weight, and activity level. To determine your caloric needs, start by estimating how active you are. A "sedentary" individual is someone who does not take part in any activity beyond that required for daily independent living, such as housework, homework, yard work, and gardening. To be in the "low active" category, an adult weighing 150 pounds would need to use an amount of energy equivalent to walking about 2 miles at 3 to 4 miles per hour in addition to the activities of daily living. To be "active," this same adult would need to perform daily exercise equivalent to walking 7 miles at a rate of 3 to 4 miles per hour, and to be "very active," he or she would need to perform the equivalent of walking 17 miles at this rate, in addition to the activities of daily living. After you have figured out your activity level, you can calculate your calorie needs using the equations in Table 10.1.

Table 10.1 Calculating Your Calorie Needs

- Determine your weight in kilograms (kg) and your height in meters (m)

    Weight in kg = weight in pounds / 2.2 pounds per kg

    Height in meters = height in inches x 0.0254 inches per m

For example:

    160 pounds = 160 lbs/2.2 lbs/kg = 72.7 kg

    5 feet 9 inches = 69 inches x 0.0254 in/m = 1.75 m

- Estimate your physical activity level and find your PA value in the table below.

LIFE STAGE	PHYSICAL ACTIVITY FACTOR (PA)			
Activity Level	**Sedentary**	**Low Active**	**Active**	**Very Active**
Boys 3–18 yrs	1	1.13	1.26	1.42
Girls 3–18 yrs	1	1.16	1.31	1.56
Men	1	1.11	1.25	1.48
Women	1	1.12	1.27	1.45

For example, if you are an active 19-year-old male, your PA value is 1.25.

- Use the appropriate EER prediction equation below to find your EER:

For example:

    If you are an active 19-year-old male,

    EER = 662 – (9.53 x Age in yrs) + PA [(15.91 x Weight in kg) + (539.6 x Height in m)]

    Where age = 19 yrs, weight = 72.7 kg, height = 1.75 m, Active PA =1.25

    EER = 662 – (9.53 x 19)+ 1.25 [(15.91 x 72.7) + (539.6 x 1.75)] = 3,107 Cal/day

LIFE STAGE	EER PREDICTION EQUATION
Boys 9–18 yrs	EER = 88.5 – (61.9 x Age in yrs) + PA [(26.7 x Weight in kg) + (903 x Height in m)] + 25
Girls 9–18 yrs	EER = 135.3 – (30.8 x Age in yrs) + PA [(10.0 x Weight in kg) + (934 x Height in m)] + 25
Men ≥19 yrs	EER = 662 – (9.53 x Age in yrs) + PA [(15.91 x Weight in kg) + (539.6 x Height in m)]
Women ≥19 yrs	EER = 354 – (6.91 x Age in yrs) + PA [(9.36 x Weight in kg) + (726 x Height in m)]

HOW MUCH EXERCISE SHOULD YOU GET?

Exercise is good for you, yet most Americans include very little activity in their daily lives. In fact, about 25% of adult Americans claim they get no physical activity at all during their leisure time.[29] A regular program of exercise increases your fitness level and makes the tasks of everyday life easier. Regular physical activity can help you keep your weight within a healthy range and can help reduce the risks of a variety of chronic diseases. It enhances fitness, strength, and flexibility; improves body composition; and contributes greatly to quality of life. Exercise also promotes psychological well-being. It helps you feel better about yourself and reduces feelings of depression and anxiety. It stimulates the release of chemicals called endorphins, which are thought to be natural tranquilizers that play a role in triggering what athletes describe as an "exercise high." In addition to causing this state of exercise euphoria, endorphins are thought to reduce anxiety, aid in relaxation, and improve mood, pain tolerance, and control appetite.

In order to get these benefits, exercise needs to be part of your daily routine. The most recent public health messages recommend 60 minutes of moderate physical activity daily.[30] This is equivalent to walking at a speed of about 3 to 4 miles per hour for one hour. The same amount of exercise can be obtained in shorter sessions of more intense activity, such as jogging or playing basketball for 30 minutes. Less exercise than this is not enough to promote the maintenance of a healthy body weight or to fully reduce chronic disease risk. Higher activity levels do not necessarily enhance other health benefits and excessive amounts of physical activity can lead to injuries, menstrual abnormalities, and bone weakening.

What Type of Exercise Is Best?

There is no one best type of exercise. As with diet, variety is key. Choose activities you enjoy and mix them up. Bike one day, swim the next, and then spend a session lifting weights at the gym. A well-planned exercise regimen includes **aerobic exercise** to improve cardiovascular and respiratory fitness, stretching to promote and maintain flexibility, and resistance training to enhance the strength and endurance of specific muscles.

Aerobic exercise includes activities such as walking, bicycling, skating, swimming, and jogging, and should be performed for about 20 to 60 minutes most days of the week. For optimal benefit, aerobic activity should be performed at a level that raises the heart rate to 60 to 85% of its maximum. Maximum heart rate is dependent on age and can be estimated by subtracting your age from 220. Therefore, a 20-year-old individual would have a maximum heart rate of 200 beats per minute and should exercise at a pace that keeps the heart rate between 120 and 170 beats per minute. A sedentary individual beginning an exercise program may find that mild exercise such as walking can raise the heart rate into this range. As fitness improves, you must perform more intense activity to raise your heart rate to this level.

To improve and maintain flexibility, stretching exercises should be done at least three days a week. Muscles should be stretched to a position of mild discomfort and held for 10 to 30 seconds. Each stretch should be repeated three to five times.

Resistance training, such as weight lifting, should be done two to three days a week at the start of an exercise program, and two days a week after the desired strength has been achieved. This can be done with weights or with resistance-exercise machines. Each session should include a minimum of 8 to 10 exercises that train the major muscle groups. Each exercise should be repeated 8 to 12 times. The weights should be heavy enough to cause the muscle to be near exhaustion after the 8 to 12 repetitions. Increasing the amount of weight lifted will increase muscle strength, whereas increasing the number of repetitions will improve endurance.

To decrease the risk of injury, each exercise session should begin with a warm-up to increase blood flow to the muscles. Warm muscles are limber, and keeping loose reduces the risk of injury and soreness. A five-minute warm-up of walking or rhythmic movement is recommended before starting any strenuous activity. A cooldown after the workout helps prevent muscle cramps and slowly brings heart rate down.

How Much Should Children and Adolescents Exercise?

Children should also spend about 60 minutes per day exercising.[30] Activity for children should be developmentally appropriate and should include periods of moderate to vigorous activity lasting 10 to 15 minutes or more, followed by periods of rest and recovery. Rather than a scheduled trip to the gym, children and adolescents should get their exercise by participating in activities with friends and family, such as bike riding, skating, skiing, throwing a ball, or building a snow fort. Most American youth do not get the recommended amount of exercise. This is because television, computers, and video games are often chosen over physical activity. Studies have found that children who watch 4 or more hours of television per day have more body fat and a greater body mass index than those who spend fewer than 2 hours watching television.[31] Children who learn to enjoy physical activity are more likely to be active adults who maintain a healthy body weight and have a lower risk of disease. Learning by example is always best. Children who have physically active parents

FACT BOX 10.4

How Much Does Activity Affect Energy Needs?

If you increase your overall level of physical activity, you need to eat more to maintain your weight. Using the EER equation shown below you can calculate that a sedentary 16-year-old girl who is 5'4" tall and weighs 127 pounds needs to eat only 1,770 Calories a day to maintain her weight. If she adds an hour of moderate activity to her day, she will be in the active PA category and will need to increase her food intake to 2,420 Calories per day to maintain her weight. If she joins the soccer team and gets 2 hours of vigorous exercise at practice every day, she will need to increase her intake to 2,940 Calories or more per day.

$$EER = 135.3-(30.8 \times \text{Age in yrs}) + PA\ [(10.0 \times \text{Weight in kg}) + (934 \times \text{Height in m})] + 25$$

PA = sedentary 1.0, low active 1.16, active 1.31, very active 1.56

are the leanest and fittest. The goal is an active lifestyle that can be continued over the long term.

FEEL GOOD ABOUT YOURSELF

If you are eating the right amounts of a variety of healthy foods and exercising regularly, you should feel good and look good. Your weight will take care of itself and your body will be toned and strong. Exercise and a healthy diet also improve your mood and your outlook on life. These are the first steps to feeling good about yourself and your body. They can't make you more beautiful, more popular, or more athletically gifted, but people who are happy with themselves are more free to enjoy life and the people and opportunities around them. If you feel good in your body, others will see you in a more positive light. This will help you develop a positive body image and reduce the risk that you will develop an eating disorder.

CONNECTIONS

A healthy lifestyle, including a nutritious diet and regular exercise, offers many health benefits. A healthy lifestyle makes it easier to maintain a safe body weight. A nutritious diet is one that provides the right number of calories to keep your weight within the desirable range; the proper balance of carbohydrates, protein, and fat choices; plenty of water; and sufficient but not excessive amounts of essential vitamins and minerals. Maintaining a healthy weight means balancing the calories you consume in your diet with the amount of energy you burn to stay alive and moving. Caloric needs can be estimated using the EER equations. A healthy exercise program requires about an hour of moderate activity daily. A good exercise regimen should include aerobic exercise, strength training, and stretching exercises. A healthy diet and regular exercise will help you feel better about yourself and decrease the risk that you will develop a poor body image and an eating disorder.

Appendices

Appendix A

Acceptable Macronutrient Distribution Ranges (AMDR) for Healthy Diets as a Percent of Energy

Age	Carbohydrate	Added sugars	Total Fat	Linoleic acid	α-Linolenic acid	Protein
1-3 y	45-65	≤25	30-40	5-10	0.6-1.2	5-20
4-18 y	45-65	≤25	25-35	5-10	0.6-1.2	10-30
≥ 19 y	45-65	≤25	20-35	5-10	0.6-1.2	10-35

Source: Institute of Medicine, Food and Nutrition Board. "Dietary Reference Intakes for Energy, Carbohydrates, Fiber, Fat, Protein, and Amino Acids." Washington, D.C.: National Academies Press, 2002.

Dietary Reference Intakes: Recommended Intakes for Individuals: Carbohydrates, Fiber, Fat, Fatty Acids, and Protein

Life Stage Group	Carbohydrate (g/day)	Fiber (g/day)	Fat (g/day)	Linoleic acid (g/day)	α-Linolenic acid (g/day)	Protein	
						(g/kg/day)	(g/day)
Infants							
0-6 mo	60*	ND	31*	4.4*†	0.5*‡	1.52*	9.1*
7-12 mo	95*	ND	30*	4.6*†	0.5*‡	1.5	13.5
Children							
1-3 y	130	19*	ND	7*	0.7*	1.10	13
4-8 y	130	25*	ND	10*	0.9*	0.95	19
Males							
9-13 y	130	31*	ND	12*	1.2*	0.95	34
14-18 y	130	38*	ND	16*	1.6*	0.85	52
19-30 y	130	38*	ND	17*	1.6*	0.80	56
31-50 y	130	38*	ND	17*	1.6*	0.80	56
51-70 y	130	30*	ND	14*	1.6*	0.80	56
> 70 y	130	30*	ND	14*	1.6*	0.80	56
Females							
9-13 y	130	26*	ND	10*	1.0*	0.95	34
14-18 y	130	26*	ND	11*	1.1*	0.85	46
19-30 y	130	25*	ND	12*	1.1*	0.80	46
31-50 y	130	25*	ND	12*	1.1*	0.80	46
51-70 y	130	21*	ND	11*	1.1*	0.80	46
> 70 y	130	21*	ND	11*	1.1*	0.80	46
Pregnancy	175	28*	ND	13*	1.4*	1.1	RDA+25g
Lactation	210	29*	ND	13*	1.3*	1.1	RDA+25g

ND = not determined
* Values are AI (adequate intakes)
† Refers to all n-6 polyunsaturated fatty acids
‡ Refers to all n-3 polyunsaturated fatty acids

Source: Institute of Medicine, Food and Nutrition Board. "Dietary Reference Intakes for Energy, Carbohydrates, Fiber, Fat, Fatty Acids, and Protein." Washington, D.C.: National Academies Press, 2002.

Dietary Reference Intake Values for Energy: Estimated Energy Requirement (EER) Equations and Values for Active Individuals by Life Stage Group

Life Stage Group	EER prediction equation	EER for Active Physical Activity Level (kcal/day)[a]	
		Male	Female
0 – 3 months	EER = (89 x weight of infant in kg – 100) + 175	538	493 (2 mo)[c]
4 – 6 months	EER = (89 x weight of infant in kg – 100) + 56	606	543 (5 mo)[c]
7 – 12 months	EER = (89 x weight of infant in kg – 100) + 22	743	676 (9 mo)[c]
1 – 2 years	EER = (89 x weight of infant in kg – 100) + 20	1046	992 (2 y)[c]
3 – 8 years			
male	EER = 88.5 – (61.9 x Age in yrs) + PA[b][(26.7 x Weight in kg) + (903 x Height in m)] + 20	1742 (6 y)[c]	
female	EER = 135.3 – (30.8 x Age in yrs) + PA[b][(10.0 x Weight in kg) + (934 x Height in m)] + 20		1642 (6 y)[c]
9 – 13 years			
male	EER = 88.5 – (61.9 x Age in yrs) + PA[b] [(26.7 x Weight in kg) + (903 x Height in m)] + 25	2279 (11 y)[c]	
female	EER = 135.3 – (30.8 x Age in yrs) + PA[b] [(10.0 x Weight in kg) + (934 x Height in m)] + 25		2071 (11 y)[c]
14 – 18 years			
male	EER = 88.5 – (61.9 x Age in yrs) + PA[b] [(26.7 x Weight in kg) + (903 x Height in m)] + 25	3152 (16 y)[c]	
female	EER = 135.3 – (30.8 x Age in yrs) + PA[b] [(10.0 x Weight in kg) + (934 x Height in m)] + 25		2368 (16 y)[c]
19 and older			
males	EER = 662 – (9.53 x Age in yrs) + PA[b][(15.91 x Weight in kg) + (539.6 x Height in m)]	3067 (19 y)[c]	
females	EER = 354 – (6.91 x Age in yrs) + PA[b][(9.36 x Weight in kg) + (726 x Height in m)]		2403 (19 y)[c]
Pregnancy			
14 –18 years			
1st trimester	Adolescent EER + 0		2368 (16 y)[c]
2nd trimester	Adolescent EER + 340 kcal		2708 (16 y)[c]
3rd trimester	Adolescent EER + 452 kcal		2820 (16 y)[c]
19 – 50 years			
1st trimester	Adult EER + 0		2403 (19 y)[c]
2nd trimester	Adult EER + 340 kcal		2743 (19 y)[c]
3rd trimester	Adult EER + 452 kcal		2855 (19 y)[c]
Lactation			
14 –18 years			
1st 6 mo	Adolescent EER + 330 kcal		2698 (16 y)[c]
2nd 6 mo	Adolescent EER + 400 kcal		2768 (16 y)[c]
19 – 50 years			
1st 6 mo	Adult EER + 330 kcal		2733 (19 y)[c]
2nd 6 mo	Adult EER + 400 kcal		2803 (19 y)[c]

[a] The intake that meets the average energy expenditure of individuals at a reference height, weight, and age.
[b] See table entitled "PA Values" to determine the PA value for various ages, genders, and activity levels.
[c] Value is calculated for an individual at the age in parentheses.

PA Values used to calculate EER

Physical Activity Level (PA)	Sedentary	Low active	Active	Very active
3 to 18 years				
Boys	1.00	1.13	1.26	1.42
Girls	1.00	1.16	1.31	1.56
≥ 19 years				
Men	1.00	1.11	1.25	1.48
Women	1.00	1.12	1.27	1.45

Source: Institute of Medicine, Food and Nutrition Board. "Dietary Reference Intakes for Energy, Carbohydrates, Fiber, Fat, Protein, and Amino Acids." Washington, D.C.: National Academies Press, 2002.

Appendix B

Dietary Reference Intakes: Recommended Intakes for Individuals: Vitamins

Life Stage Group	Vitamin A (µg/day)[a]	Vitamin C (mg/day)	Vitamin D (µg/day)[b,c]	Vitamin E (mg/day)[d]	Vitamin K (µg/day)	Thiamin (mg/day)	Riboflavin (mg/day)	Niacin (mg/day)[e]	Vitamin B6 (mg/day)	Folate (µg/day)[f]	Vitamin B12 (µg/day)	Pantothenic Acid (mg/day)	Biotin (µg/day)	Choline[g] (mg/day)
Infants														
0-6 mo	400*	40*	5*	4*	2.0*	0.2*	0.3*	2*	0.1*	65*	0.4*	1.7*	5*	125*
7-12 mo	500*	50*	5*	5*	2.5*	0.3*	0.4*	4*	0.3*	80*	0.5*	1.8*	6*	150*
Children														
1-3 y	**300**	**15**	5*	**6**	30*	**0.5**	**0.5**	**6**	**0.5**	**150**	**0.9**	2*	8*	200*
4-8 y	**400**	**25**	5*	**7**	55*	**0.6**	**0.6**	**8**	**0.5**	**200**	**1.2**	3*	12*	250*
Males														
9-13 y	**600**	**45**	5*	**11**	60*	**0.9**	**0.9**	**12**	**1.0**	**300**	**1.8**	4*	20*	315*
14-18 y	**900**	**75**	5*	**15**	75*	**1.2**	**1.3**	**16**	**1.3**	**400**	**2.4**	5*	25*	550*
19-30 y	**900**	**90**	5*	**15**	120*	**1.2**	**1.3**	**16**	**1.3**	**400**	**2.4**	5*	30*	550*
31-50 y	**900**	**90**	5*	**15**	120*	**1.2**	**1.3**	**16**	**1.3**	**400**	**2.4**	5*	30*	550*
51-70 y	**900**	**90**	10*	**15**	120*	**1.2**	**1.3**	**16**	**1.7**	**400**	**2.4**[h]	5*	30*	550*
> 70 y	**900**	**90**	15*	**15**	120*	**1.2**	**1.3**	**16**	**1.7**	**400**	**2.4**[h]	5*	30*	550*
Females														
9-13 y	**600**	**45**	5*	**11**	60*	**0.9**	**0.9**	**12**	**1.0**	**300**	**1.8**	4*	20*	375*
14-18 y	**700**	**65**	5*	**15**	75*	**1.0**	**1.0**	**14**	**1.2**	**400**[i]	**2.4**	5*	25*	400*
19-30 y	**700**	**75**	5*	**15**	90*	**1.1**	**1.1**	**14**	**1.3**	**400**[i]	**2.4**	5*	30*	425*
31-50 y	**700**	**75**	5*	**15**	90*	**1.1**	**1.1**	**14**	**1.3**	**400**[i]	**2.4**	5*	30*	425*
51-70 y	**700**	**75**	10*	**15**	90*	**1.1**	**1.1**	**14**	**1.5**	**400**	**2.4**[h]	5*	30*	425*
> 70 y	**700**	**75**	15*	**15**	90*	**1.1**	**1.1**	**14**	**1.5**	**400**	**2.4**[h]	5*	30*	425*
Pregnancy														
≤ 18 y	**750**	**80**	5*	**15**	75*	**1.4**	**1.4**	**18**	**1.9**	**600**[j]	**2.6**	6*	30*	450*
14-18 y	**770**	**85**	5*	**15**	90*	**1.4**	**1.4**	**18**	**1.9**	**600**[j]	**2.6**	6*	30*	450*
19-30 y	**770**	**85**	5*	**15**	90*	**1.4**	**1.4**	**18**	**1.9**	**600**[j]	**2.6**	6*	30*	450*
Lactation														
≤ 18 y	**1200** .	**115**	5*	**19**	75*	**1.4**	**1.6**	**17**	**2.0**	**500**	**2.8**	7*	35*	550*
14-18 y	**1300**	**120**	5*	**19**	90*	**1.4**	**1.6**	**17**	**2.0**	**500**	**2.8**	7*	35*	550*
19-30 y	**1300**	**120**	5*	**19**	90*	**1.4**	**1.6**	**17**	**2.0**	**500**	**2.8**	7*	35*	550*

NOTE: This table (taken from the DRI reports, see www.nap.edu) presents Recommended Dietary Allowances (RDAs) in **bold** type and Adequate Intakes (AIs) in ordinary type followed by an asterisk (*). RDAs and AIs may both be used as goals for individual intakes. RDAs are set up to meet the needs of almost all (97–98%) individuals in a group. For healthy breastfed infants, the AI is the mean intake. The AI for all other life stage and gender groups is believed to cover needs of all individuals in the group, but lack of data or uncertainty in the data prevent being able to specify with confidence the percentage of individuals covered by this intake.

[a]As retinol activity equivalents (RAEs). 1 RAE = 1 µg retinol, 12 µg β-carotene, 24 µg β-carotene, or 24 µg β-cryptoxanthin in foods. To calculate RAEs from REs of provitamin A carotenoids in foods, divide RE by 2. For preformed vitamin A in foods or supplements and for provitamin A carotenoids in supplements, 1 RE = 1 RAE.

[b]Cholecalciferol. 1 µg cholecalciferol = 40 IU vitamin D.

[c]In the absence of exposure to adequate sunlight.

[d]As α-tocopherol, which includes RRR-α-tocopherol, the only form of α-tocopherol that occurs naturally in foods, and the 2R-stereoisomeric forms of α-tocopherol (RRR-, RSR-, RRS-, and RSS-α-tocopherol). Does not include the 2S-stereoisomeric forms of α-tocopherol (SRR-, SSR-, SRS-, and SSS- α -tocopherol), also found in food and supplements.

[e]As niacin equivalents (NEs), 1mg niacin = 60 mg tryptophan; 0-6 months = preformed niacin (not NE).

[f]As dietary folate equivalents (DFEs). 1 DFE = 1 µg food folate = 0.6 µg folic acid from fortified food or as a supplement consumed with food = 0.5 µg of a supplement taken on an empty stomach.

[g]Although AIs have been set for choline, there are few data to assess whether a dietary supplement of choline is needed at all stages of the life cycle, and it may be that the choline requirement can be met by endogenous synthesis at some of these stages.

[h]Because 10-30% of older people may malabsorb food-bound B12, it is advisable for those older than 50 years to meet their RFD mainly by consuming foods fortified with B12 or containing B12.

[i]In view of evidence linking folate intake with neural tube defects in the fetus, it is recommended that all women capable of becoming pregnant consume 400 µg from supplements or fortified foods in addition to intake of food folate from a varied diet.

[j]It is assumed that women will consume 400 µg from supplements or fortified foods until their pregnancy is confirmed and they enter prenatal care, which ordinarily occurs after the end of the periconceptional period – the critical time for neural tube formation.

Source: Trumbo, P., A. Yates, S. Schlicker, M. Poos. "Dietary Reference Intakes: Vitamin A, Vitamin K, Arsenic, Boron, Chromium, Copper, Iodine, Iron, Manganese, Molybdenum, Nickel, Silicon, Vanadium, and Zinc." *Journal of the American Dietetic Association* 101, no. 3 (2001) 294-301.

Dietary Reference Intakes: Recommended Intakes for Individuals: Minerals

Life Stage Group	Calcium (mg/day)	Chromium (µg/day)	Copper (µg/day)	Fluoride (mg/day)	Iodine (µg/day)	Iron (mg/day)	Magnesium (mg/day)	Manganese (mg/day)	Molybdenum (µg/day)	Phosphorus (mg/day)	Selenium (µg/day)	Zinc (mg/day)
Infants												
0-6 mo	210*	0.2*	200*	0.01*	110*	0.27*	30*	0.003*	2*	100*	15*	2*
7-12 mo	270*	5.5*	220*	0.5*	130*	11	75*	0.6*	3*	275*	20*	3
Children												
1-3 y	500*	11*	340	0.7*	90	7	80	1.2*	17	460	20	3
4-8 y	800*	15*	440	1*	90	10	130	1.5*	22	500	30	5
Males												
9-13 y	1,300*	25*	700	2*	120	8	240	1.9*	34	1,250	40	8
14-18 y	1,300*	35*	890	3*	150	11	410	2.2*	43	1,250	55	11
19-30 y	1,000*	35*	900	4*	150	8	400	2.3*	45	700	55	11
31-50 y	1,000*	35*	900	4*	150	8	420	2.3*	45	700	55	11
51-70 y	1,200*	30*	900	4*	150	8	420	2.3*	45	700	55	11
>70 y	1,200*	30*	900	4*	150	8	420	2.3*	45	700	55	11
Females												
9-13 y	1,300*	21*	700	2*	120	8	240	1.6*	34	1,250	40	8
14-18 y	1,300*	24*	890	3*	150	15	360	1.6*	43	1,250	55	9
19-30 y	1,000*	25*	900	3*	150	18	310	1.8*	45	700	55	8
31-50 y	1,000*	25*	900	3*	150	18	320	1.8*	45	700	55	8
51-70 y	1,200*	20*	900	3*	150	8	320	1.8*	45	700	55	8
>70 y	1,200*	20*	900	3*	150	8	320	1.8*	45	700	55	8
Pregnancy												
≤18 y	1,300*	29*	1,000	3*	220	27	400	2.0*	50	1,250	60	13
14-18 y	1,000*	30*	1,000	3*	220	27	350	2.0*	50	700	60	11
19-30 y	1,000*	30*	1,000	3*	220	27	360	2.0*	50	700	60	11
Lactation												
≤18 y	1,300*	44*	1,300	3*	290	10	360	2.6*	50	1,250	70	14
14-18 y	1,300*	45*	1,300	3*	290	9	310	2.6*	50	700	70	12
19-30 y	1,300*	45*	1,300	3*	290	9	320	2.6*	50	700	70	12

NOTE: This table (taken from the DRI reports, see www.nap.edu) presents Recommended Dietary Allowances (RDAs) in **bold** type and Adequate Intakes (AIs) in ordinary type followed by an asterisk (*). RDAs and AIs may both be used as goals for individual intakes. RDAs are set up to meet the needs of almost all (97-98%) individuals in a group. For healthy breastfed infants, the AI is the mean intake. The AI for all other life stage and gender groups is believed to cover needs of all individuals in the group, but lack of data or uncertainty in the data prevents being able to specify with confidence the percentage of individuals covered by this intake.

Dietary Reference Intakes (DRIs): Tolerable Upper Intake Levels (UL[a]): Vitamins

Life Stage Group	Vitamin A (µg/day)[b]	Vitamin C (mg/day)	Vitamin D (µg/day)	Vitamin E (mg/day)[c,d]	Vitamin K	Thiamin	Riboflavin	Niacin (mg/day)[d]	Vitamin B$_6$ (mg/day)	Folate (µg/day)[d]	Vitamin B$_{12}$	Pantothenic Acid	Biotin	Choline (mg/day)	Carotenoids[e]
Infants															
0-6 mo	600	ND[f]	25	ND[f]	ND	ND	ND	ND	ND	ND	ND	ND	ND	ND	ND
7-12 mo	600	ND	25	ND	ND	ND	ND	ND	ND	ND	ND	ND	ND	ND	ND
Children															
1-3 y	600	400	50	200	ND	ND	ND	10	30	300	ND	ND	ND	1.0	ND
4-8 y	900	650	50	300	ND	ND	ND	15	40	400	ND	ND	ND	1.0	ND
Males, Females															
9-13 y	1,700	1,200	50	600	ND	ND	ND	20	60	600	ND	ND	ND	2.0	ND
14-18 y	2,800	1,800	50	800	ND	ND	ND	30	80	800	ND	ND	ND	3.0	ND
19-70 y	3,000	2,000	50	1,000	ND	ND	ND	35	100	1,000	ND	ND	ND	3.5	ND
>70 y	3,000	2,000	50	1,000	ND	ND	ND	35	100	1,000	ND	ND	ND	3.5	ND
Pregnancy															
≤18 y	2,800	1,800	50	800	ND	ND	ND	30	80	800	ND	ND	ND	3.0	ND
19-50 y	3,000	2,000	50	1,000	ND	ND	ND	35	100	1,000	ND	ND	ND	3.5	ND
Lactation															
≤18 y	2,800	1,800	50	800	ND	ND	ND	30	80	800	ND	ND	ND	3.0	ND
19-50 y	3,000	2,000	50	1,000	ND	ND	ND	35	100	1,000	ND	ND	ND	3.5	ND

[a]UL = The maximum level of daily nutrient intake that is likely to pose no risk of adverse effects. Unless otherwise specified, the UL represents total intake from food, water, and supplements. Due to lack of suitable data, ULs could not be established for vitamin K, thiamin, riboflavin, vitamin B$_{12}$, pantothenic acid, biotin, or carotenoids. In the absence of ULs, extra caution may be warranted in consuming levels above recommended intakes.

[b]As preformed vitamin A only.

[c]As α-tocopherol; applies to any for of supplemental α-tocopherol.

[d]The ULs for vitamin E, niacin, and folate apply to synthetic forms obtained from supplements, fortified foods, or a combination of the two.

[e]β-Carotene supplements are advised only to serve as a provitamin A source for individuals at risk of vitamin A deficiency.

[f]ND=Not determinable due to lack of data of adverse effects in this age group and concern with regard to lack of ability to handle excess amounts. Source of intakes should be from food only to prevent high levels of intake.

Dietary Reference Intakes (DRIs): Tolerable Upper Intake Levels (UL[a]): Minerals

Life Stage Group	Arsenic[b]	Boron (mg/day)	Calcium (g/day)	Chromium	Copper (µg/day)	Fluoride (mg/day)	Iodine (µg/day)	Iron (mg/day)	Magnesium (mg/day)[c]	Manganese (mg/day)	Molybdenum (µg/day)	Nickel (mg/day)	Phosphorus (g/day)	Selenium (µg/day)	Silicon[d]	Vanadium (mg/day)[e]	Zinc (mg/day)
Infants																	
0-6 mo	ND[f]	ND	ND	ND	ND	0.7	ND	40	ND	ND	ND	ND	ND	45	ND	ND	4
7-12 mo	ND	ND	ND	ND	ND	0.9	ND	40	ND	ND	ND	ND	ND	60	ND	ND	5
Children																	
1-3 y	ND	3	2.5	ND	1,000	1.3	200	40	65	2	300	0.2	3	90	ND	ND	7
4-8 y	ND	6	2.5	ND	3,000	2.2	300	40	110	3	600	0.3	3	150	ND	ND	12
Males, Females																	
9-13 y	ND	11	2.5	ND	5,000	10	600	40	350	6	1,100	0.6	4	280	ND	ND	23
14-18 y	ND	17	2.5	ND	8,000	10	900	45	350	9	1,700	1.0	4	400	ND	ND	34
19-70 y	ND	20	2.5	ND	10,000	10	1,100	45	350	11	2,000	1.0	4	400	ND	1.8	40
>70 y	ND	20	2.5	ND	10,000	10	1,100	45	350	11	2,000	1.0	3	400	ND	1.8	40
Pregnancy																	
≤18 y	ND	17	2.5	ND	8,000	10	900	45	350	9	1,700	1.0	3.5	400	ND	ND	34
19-50 y	ND	20	2.5	ND	10,000	10	1,100	45	350	11	2,000	1.0	3.5	400	ND	ND	40
Lactation																	
≤18 y	ND	17	2.5	ND	8,000	10	900	45	350	9	1,700	1.0	4	400	ND	ND	34
19-50 y	ND	20	2.5	ND	10,000	10	1,100	45	350	11	2,000	1.0	4	400	ND	ND	40

aUL= the maximum level of daily nutrient intake that is likely to pose no risk of adverse effects. Unless otherwise specified, the UL represents total intake from food, water, and supplements. Due to lack of suitable data, ULs could not be established for arsenic, chromium, and silicon. In the absence of ULs, extra caution may be warranted in consuming levels above recommended intakes.

bAlthough the UL was not determined for arsenic, there is no justification for adding arsenic to food or supplements.

cThe ULs for magnesium represent intake from a pharmacological agent only and do not include intake from food and water.

dAlthough silicon has not been shown to cause adverse effects in humans, there is no justification for adding silicon to supplements.

eAlthough vanadium in food has not been shown to cause adverse effects in humans, there is no justification for adding vanadium to food and vanadium supplements should be used with caution. The UL is based on adverse effects in laboratory animals and this data could be used to set a UL for adults but not children and adolescents.

fND=Not determinable due to lack of data of adverse effects in this age group and concern with regard to lack of ability to handle excess amounts. Source of intake should be from food only to prevent high levels of intake.

Appendix B

Dietary Reference Intakes: Recommended Intakes and Tolerable Upper Intake Levels (UL): Water, Potassium, Sodium, and Chloride						
Life Stage Group	Water [a] (liters)	Potassium [a,b] (mg)	Sodium (mg)		Chloride (mg)	
			Recommended Intake	UL	Recommended Intake	UL
Infants						
0–6 mo	0.7	0.4	0.12	-	0.18	-
7–12 mo	0.8	0.7	0.37	-	0.58	-
Children						
1–3 y	1.3	3.0	1.0	1.5	1.5	2.3
4–8 y	1.7	3.8	1.2	1.9	1.9	2.9
Males						
9–13 y	2.4	4.5	1.5	2.2	2.3	3.4
14–18 y	3.3	4.7	1.5	2.3	2.3	3.6
19–30 y	3.7	4.7	1.5	2.3	2.3	3.6
31–50 y	3.7	4.7	1.5	2.3	2.3	3.6
51–70 y	3.7	4.7	1.3	2.3	2.0	3.6
>70 y	3.7	4.7	1.2	2.3	1.8	3.6
Females						
9–13 y	2.1	4.5	1.5	2.2	2.3	3.4
14–18 y	2.3	4.7	1.5	2.3	2.3	3.6
19–30 y	2.7	4.7	1.5	2.3	2.3	3.6
31–50 y	2.7	4.7	1.5	2.3	2.3	3.6
51–70 y	2.7	4.7	1.3	2.3	2.0	3.6
>70 y	2.7	4.7	1.2	2.3	1.8	3.6

[a] No UL has been established for water or potassium.

[b] The recommended intake is the same for all groups over 14 years except lactating women, which is 5.1 mg.

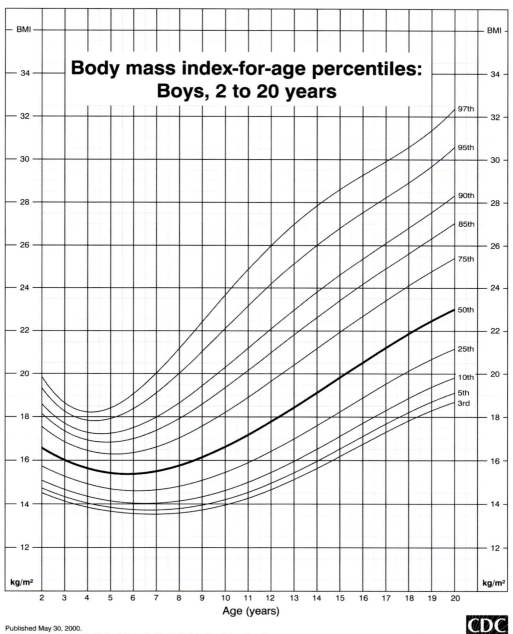

Body mass index-for-age percentiles: Boys, 2 to 20 years

Published May 30, 2000.
SOURCE: Developed by the National Center for Health Statistics in collaboration with
the National Center for Chronic Disease Prevention and Health Promotion (2000).

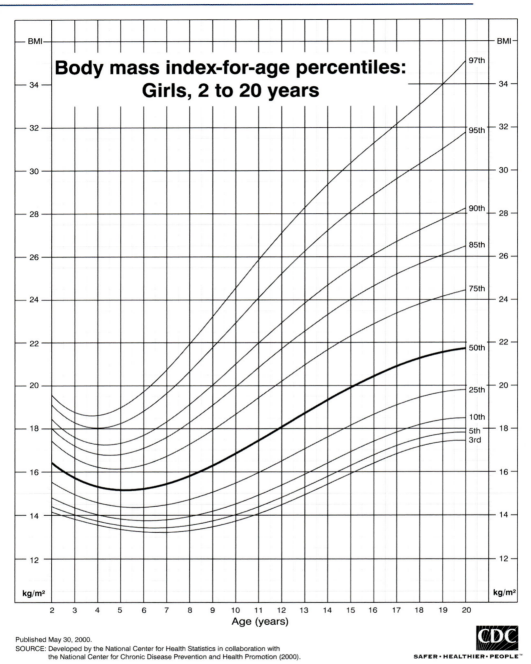

**Body mass index-for-age percentiles:
Girls, 2 to 20 years**

Published May 30, 2000.
SOURCE: Developed by the National Center for Health Statistics in collaboration with
the National Center for Chronic Disease Prevention and Health Promotion (2000).

SAFER · HEALTHIER · PEOPLE™

Glossary

Absorption The process of taking substances into the interior of the body.

Adenosine triphosphate (ATP) The high-energy molecule used by the body to perform energy-requiring activities.

Adequate Intakes (AIs) Intakes recommended by the DRIs that should be used as a goal when no RDA exists. These values are an approximation of the average nutrient intake that appears to sustain a desired indicator of health.

Aerobic exercise Exercise that uses aerobic metabolism, which uses oxygen and improves cardiovascular fitness.

Amenorrhea Absence or abnormal cessation of menstrual periods in women.

Amino acids The building blocks of proteins. Each contains a carbon atom bound to a hydrogen atom, an amino group, an acid group, and a side chain.

Anorexia nervosa An eating disorder characterized by a distorted body image, self-starvation, and loss of 15% or more of normal weight for age and height.

Antioxidant A substance that is able to neutralize reactive molecules and hence reduce the amount of oxidative damage that occurs.

Appetite A drive to eat specific foods that is not necessarily related to hunger.

ATP See **adenosine triphosphate**.

Binge Consumption of an abnormally large amount of food in a relatively short period of time.

Binge-eating disorder An eating disorder characterized by binge eating that is not followed by compensatory purging.

Body image The way a person perceives or imagines his or her body.

Body mass index (BMI) The currently accepted measure for evaluating desirable body weight. It is calculated by dividing weight in pounds by the square of height in inches ($height^2$) and multiplying the dividend by 703.

Bulimia nervosa An eating disorder characterized by repeated cycles of binging and purging.

Calorie The amount of heat needed to raise one gram of water 1°C (34°F). It is commonly used to refer to a kilocalorie, which is 1,000 calories.

Cholesterol A lipid made only by animal cells that consists of multiple chemical rings.

Glossary

Daily Value A nutrient reference value used on food labels to help consumers see how foods fit into their overall diets.

Diabetes A disease caused by either insufficient insulin production or decreased sensitivity of cells to insulin. It results in elevated blood glucose levels.

Dietary References Intakes (DRIs) A set of four reference values for the intake of nutrients and food components that can be used for planning and assessing the diets of healthy people in the United States and Canada.

Digestion The process of breaking food into components small enough to be absorbed into the body.

Eating disorder A group of conditions characterized by a pathological concern with body weight and shape.

Eating disorders not otherwise specified (EDNOS) Eating disorders that do not meet the defining criteria of anorexia or bulimia.

Elements Substances that cannot be broken down into products with different properties.

Enzymes Protein molecules that accelerate the rate of specific chemical reactions without being changed themselves.

Essential nutrients Nutrients that must be supplied in the diet because they cannot be made in sufficient quantities in the body to meet needs.

Estimated Average Requirements (EARs) Intakes recommended by the DRIs that meet the estimated nutrient needs (as defined by a specific indicator of adequacy) of 50% of individuals in a particular gender and life-stage group.

Estimated Energy Requirements (EERs) Energy intakes recommended by the DRIs to maintain body weight.

Extreme obesity A condition in which body weight is 100 pounds (45 kg) above healthy body weight or body mass index is greater than 40 kg/m^2; also called **morbid obesity**.

Fatty acid An organic molecule made up of a chain of carbons linked to hydrogens with an acid group at one end.

Fiber Nonstarch polysaccharides in plant foods that are not broken down by human digestive enzymes.

Fortification The addition of nutrients to foods, such as the addition of vitamin D to milk.

Free radical One type of highly reactive molecule that causes oxidative damage.

Gene A section of DNA that codes for a protein.

Homeostasis A physiological state in which a stable internal body environment is maintained.

Hormones Chemical messengers that are produced in one location, released into the blood, and elicit responses at other locations in the body.

Hunger The physiological drive to consume food.

Kilocalorie A unit of heat that is used to express the amount of energy provided by foods. It is commonly called a Calorie.

Kilojoule A measure of work that can be used to express energy intake and energy output; 4.18 kjoules = 1 kcalorie.

Lanugo hair Abnormal fine hair that grows all over the body. It is a symptom of anorexia nervosa.

Lean body mass The proportion of body mass that is not fat.

Macronutrients Nutrients needed by the body in relatively large amounts. These include water, carbohydrates, fats, and protein.

Malnutrition Any condition resulting from an energy or nutrient intake either above or below that which is optimal.

Metabolism The sum of all the chemical reactions that take place in a living organism.

Micronutrients Nutrients needed by the body in small amounts. These include vitamins and minerals.

Morbid obesity See **extreme obesity**.

Mucus A viscous fluid secreted by glands in the gastrointestinal tract and other parts of the body. It acts to lubricate, moisten, and protect cells from harsh environments.

Neurotransmitter A chemical substance produced by a nerve cell that can stimulate or inhibit another cell.

Night-eating syndrome An eating disorder that involves lack of hunger in the morning, followed by insomnia and excessive eating at night.

Nutrient density A measure of the nutrients provided by a food relative to the energy it contains.

Nutrients Chemical substances in foods that provide energy, structure, and regulation for body processes.

Glossary

Nutrition The science that studies the interactions that occur between living organisms and food.

Obese Having a body mass index of greater than or equal to 30 kg/m².

Organic molecules Molecules containing 2 or more carbon atoms in their structure.

Overnutrition Poor nutritional status resulting from a dietary intake in excess of that which is optimal for health.

Overweight In adults, having a body mass index greater than or equal to 25 kg/m².

Phytochemical A substance found in plant foods that is not an essential nutrient but may have health-promoting properties.

Purge An abnormal compensatory behavior used to rid the body of calories; it may include self-induced vomiting, excessive exercise, or the misuse of laxative or diuretics.

Recommended Dietary Allowances (RDAs) Intakes recommended by the DRIs that are sufficient to meet the nutrient needs of almost all healthy people in a specific life-stage and gender group.

Satiety The feeling of fullness and satisfaction that follows food intake.

Saturated fat or **saturated fatty acid** A fatty acid in which the carbon atoms are bound to as many hydrogens as possible and which therefore contains no carbon-carbon double bonds.

Self-esteem The sum of how a person feels about him- or herself and abilities. It is a general attitude of approval or disapproval that indicates if the person thinks he or she is worthy and capable.

Starch A carbohydrate made of many glucose molecules linked in straight or branching chains. The bonds that hold the glucose molecules together can be broken by the human digestive enzymes.

Subcutaneous fat Body fat that is located under the skin.

Tolerable Upper Intake Level (UL) The maximum daily intake by an individual that is unlikely to pose risks of adverse health effects to almost all individuals in a specified life-stage and gender group.

Triglyceride The major form of lipid in food and in the body. It consists of three fatty acids attached to a glycerol molecule.

Underweight In adults, having a body mass index of less than 18.5 kg/m².

Unsaturated fat or **unsaturated fatty acid** A fatty acid that contains one or more carbon-carbon double bonds.

Visceral fat Body fat that is located around internal organs.

References

1. Sylvester, G.P., C. Achterberg, and J. Williams. "Children's television and nutrition." *Nutrition Today* 30 (1995): 6–15.

2. Woods, S.C., R.J. Seeley, D. Porte, and M.W. Schwartz. "Signals that regulate food intake and energy homeostasis." *Science* 280 (1998): 1378–1383.

3. Anderson, G.H. "Regulation of food intake." *Modern Nutrition in Health and Disease*, 8th ed., eds. M.E. Shils, J.A. Olson, and M. Shike. Philadelphia: Lea & Febiger, 1994, pp. 524–536.

4. Cummings, D.E., D.S. Weigle, R.S. Frayo, et al. "Plasma ghrelin levels after diet-induced weight loss or gastric bypass surgery." *New England Journal of Medicine* 346 (2002): 1623–1630.

5. Batterham, R.L., M.A. Cowley, C.J. Small, et al. "Gut hormone PYY (3-36) physiologically inhibits food intake." *Nature* 418 (2002): 650–654.

6. Institute of Medicine, Food and Nutrition Board. "Dietary Reference Intakes for Energy, Carbohydrates, Fiber, Fat, Protein, and Amino Acids." Washington, D.C.: National Academies Press, 2002.

7. American Anorexia Bulimia Association, Inc. Available online at *http://www.aabainc.org/general/index.html.*

8. Crago, M., C.M. Shisslak, and L.S. Estes. "Eating disturbances among American minority groups: A review." *International Journal of Eating Disorders* 19 (1996): 239–248.

9. Hsu, L.K. "Epidemiology of the eating disorders." *The Psychiatric Clinics of North America* 19 (1996): 681–700.

10. ANRED, Anorexia and Related Eating Disorders. "Statistics: How many people have eating disorders?" Available online at *http://www.anred.com/stats.html.*

11. American Psychiatric Association. "Practice Guidelines for the treatment of patients with eating disorders." 2000. Available online at *http://www.psych.org/clin_res/guide.bk42301.cfm.*

12. Strober, M., and C.M. Bulik. "Genetic epidemiology of eating disorders." *Eating Disorders and Obesity: A Comprehensive Handbook,* 2nd ed., eds. C.G. Fairburn and K.D. Brownell. New York: The Guilford Press, 2002, pp. 238–242.

13. Walsh, B.T., and M.J. Devlin. "Eating disorders: Progress and problems." *Science* 280 (1998): 1387–1390.

14. Branson, R.N. Potoczna, J.G. Kral, K.U. Lentes, M.R. Hoehe, and F.F. Horber. "Binge eating as a major phenotype of melanocortin 4 receptor gene mutations." *New England Journal of Medicine* 348 (2003): 1096–1103.

15. Stice, E. "Sociocultural influences on body weight and eating disturbance." *Eating Disorders and Obesity: A Comprehensive Handbook,* 2nd ed., eds. C.G. Fairburn and K.D. Brownell. New York: The Guilford Press, 2002, pp. 103–107.

16. ANAD (Anorexia Nervosa and Associated Disorders) newsletter, Summer 2001.

17. Brown, P.J., and M. Konner. "An anthropological perspective on obesity." *Human obesity*, eds. R.J. Wurtman and J.J. Wurtman. *Annals of the New York Academy of Sciences* 499 (1987): 29–46.

References

18. Office of the Surgeon General. *The Surgeon General's Call to Action to Prevent and Decrease Overweight and Obesity.* Rockville, MD: U.S. Department of Health and Human Services, 2001. Available online at *http://www.surgeongeneral.gov/topics/obesity.*

19. Foreyt, J.P., W.S.C. Poston II, and G.K. Goodrick. "Future directions in obesity and eating disorders." *Addictive Behaviors* 21 (1996): 767–778.

20. American Psychiatric Association. *Diagnostic and Statistical Manual of Mental Disorders,* 4th ed. Washington, D.C.: American Psychiatric Association, 1994.

21. Keys, A., J. Brozek, A. Henschel, et al. *The Biology of Human Starvation,* vols. 1 and 2. Minneapolis: University of Minnesota Press, 1950.

22. Vandereycken, W. "History of Anorexia Nervosa and Bulimia Nervosa." *Eating Disorders and Obesity: A Comprehensive Handbook,* 2nd ed., eds. C.G. Fairburn and K.D. Brownell. New York: The Guilford Press, 2002, pp. 151–154.

23. Kaye, W.H., T.E. Weltzin, M. McKee, et al. "Laboratory assessment of feeding behavior in bulimia nervosa and healthy women. Methods of developing a human feeding laboratory." *American Journal of Clinical Nutrition* 52 (1992): 8000–8007.

24. Herzog, D.B., D.N. Greenwood, D.J. Dorer, et al. "Mortality in eating disorders: A descriptive study." *International Journal of Eating Disorders* 28 (2000): 20–26.

25. Keel, P.K., J.E. Mitchell, K.B. Miller, et al. "Long-term outcome of bulimia nervosa." *Archives of General Psychiatry* 56 (1999): 63–69.

26. American Dietetic Association. "Position of the American Dietetic Association: Nutrition intervention in the treatment of anorexia nervosa, bulimia nervosa and eating disorders not otherwise specified (EDNOS)." *Journal of the American Dietetic Association* 101 (2001): 810–818.

27. Birketvedt, G., J. Florholmen, J. Sundsfjord, et al. "Behavioral and neuroendocrine characteristics of the night-eating syndrome." *Journal of the American Medical Association* 282 (1999): 657–663.

28. Brownell, K.D., and M.A. Napolitano. "Distorting reality for children: body size proportions of Barbie and Ken dolls." *International Journal of Eating Disorders* 3 (1995): 295–298.

29. U.S. Department of Health and Human Services. "Physical Activity and Health: A Report of the Surgeon General." Centers for Disease Control and Prevention, 1996.

30. U.S. Department of Agriculture, U.S. Department of Health and Human Services. *Nutrition and Your Health: Dietary Guidelines for Americans,* 5th ed. Home and Garden Bulletin, No. 232. Hyattsville, MD: U.S. Government Printing Office, 2000.

31. Andersen, R.E., C.J. Crespo, S.J. Bartlett, et al. "Relationship of physical activity and television watching with body weight and level of fatness among children: Results from the Third National Health and Examination Survey." *Journal of the American Medical Association* 279 (1998): 938–942.

GENERAL NUTRITION

American Dietetic Association. "Americans' Food and Nutrition Attitudes and Behaviors—Nutrition and You: Trends 2000." Available online at *http://www.eatright.org/pr/2000/010300a.html*.

Cleveland, L.E., A.J. Cook, J.W. Wilson, et al. "Pyramid Servings Data Results from the USDA's CSFII, ARS Food Surveys Research Group." Available online at *http://www.barc.usda.gov/bhnrc/foodsurvey/home/htm*.

Food and Drug Administration, Center for Food Safety and Applied Nutrition. "A Food Labeling Guide." Appendix C, Health Claims, August 12, 1997. Available online at *http://vm.cfsan.fda.gov*.

Food and Nutrition Board, Institute of Medicine. *Dietary Reference Intakes for Calcium, Phosphorus, Magnesium, Vitamin D, and Fluoride.* Washington, D.C.: National Academies Press, 1997.

———. *Dietary Reference Intakes for Energy, Carbohydrates, Fiber, Fat, Protein, and Amino Acids.* Washington, D.C.: National Academies Press, 2002.

———. *Dietary Reference Intakes for Thiamin, Riboflavin, Niacin, Vitamin B-6, Folate, Vitamin B-12, Pantothenic Acid, Biotin, and Choline.* Washington, D.C.: National Academies Press, 1998.

———. *Dietary Reference Intakes for Vitamin A, Vitamin K, Arsenic, Boron, Chromium, Copper, Iodine, Iron, Manganese, Molybdenum, Nickel, Silicon, Vanadium, and Zinc.* Washington, D.C.: National Academies Press, 2001.

———. *Dietary Reference Intakes for Vitamin C, Vitamin E, Selenium, and Carotenoids.* Washington, D.C.: National Academies Press, 2000.

Sarubin, A. *The Health Professional's Guide to Popular Dietary Supplements.* Chicago: American Dietetic Association; 2000.

Shils, M.E., J.A. Olson, and M. Shike, eds. *Modern Nutrition in Health and Disease*, 8th ed. Philadelphia: Lea & Febiger, 1994.

U.S. Department of Agriculture. "The Food Guide Pyramid." Home and Garden Bulletin No. 252. Hyattsville, MD: Human Nutrition Information Service, 1992, slightly revised, 1996.

U.S. Department of Agriculture, U.S. Department of Health and Human Services. *Nutrition and Your Health: Dietary Guidelines for Americans*, 5th ed., Item Number 147-G. Hyattsville, MD: U.S. Government Printing Office, 2000.

Further Reading

EATING DISORDERS

American Dietetic Association. "Position of the American Dietetic Association: Nutrition intervention in the treatment of anorexia nervosa, bulimia nervosa and eating disorders not otherwise specified (EDNOS)." *Journal of the American Dietetic Association* 101 (2001): 810–818.

American Psychiatric Association. *Diagnostic and Statistical Manual for Mental Disorders, fourth edition (DSM-IV)*. Washington, D.C.: American Psychiatric Press, 1994.

American Psychiatric Association Work Group on Eating Disorders. "Practice guideline for the treatment of patients with eating disorders (revision)." *American Journal of Psychiatry* 157(1, Suppl) (2000): 1–39.

ANRED, Anorexia and Related Eating Disorders. "Statistics: How many people have eating disorders?" Available online at *http://www.anred.com/stats.html*.

Apple, R.F., and W.S. Agras. *Overcoming eating disorders. A cognitive-behavioral treatment for bulimia and binge-eating disorder*. San Antonio: Harcourt Brace & Company, 1997.

Brownell, K.D., and C.G. Fairburn, eds. *Eating Disorders and Obesity: A Comprehensive Handbook*, 2nd ed. New York: The Guilford Press, 2002.

Walsh, B.T., and M.J. Devlin. "Eating disorders: Progress and problems." *Science* 280 (1998): 1387–1390.

WEIGHT MANAGEMENT

Centers for Disease Control and Prevention. *Obesity and Overweight: A Public Health Epidemic*. Available online at *http://www.cdc.gov/nccdphp/dnpa/obesity/epidemic.htm*.

National Institutes of Health, National Heart, Lung, and Blood Institute. "Clinical guidelines on the identification, evaluation, and treatment of overweight and obesity in adults." Executive summary, June 1998. Available online at *http://www.nhlbi.nih.gov/guidelines/obesity/ob_home.htm*.

National Research Council. *Diet and Health: Implications for Reducing Chronic Disease Risk*. Washington, D.C.: National Academies Press, 1989.

Office of the Surgeon General. *The Surgeon General's Call to Action to Prevent and Decrease Overweight and Obesity*. Rockville, MD: U.S. Department of Health and Human Services, 2001. Available online at *http://www.surgeongeneral.gov/topics/obesity*.

EXERCISE BENEFITS AND RECOMMENDATIONS

American College of Sports Medicine. "Position Stand on the recommended quantity and quality of exercise for developing and maintaining cardiorespiratory and muscular fitness and flexibility in adults." *Medicine and Science in Sports and Exercise* 30 (1998): 975–991.

American Dietetic Association. "Timely statement of the American Dietetic Association: Nutrition guidance for child athletes in organized sports." *Journal of the American Dietetic Association* 96 (1996): 610–611.

Haennel, R.G., and F. Lemire. "Physical activity to prevent cardiovascular disease. How much is enough?" *Canadian Family Physician* 48 (2002): 65–71

Position of the American Dietetic Association, Dietitians of Canada, and the American College of Sports Medicine. "Nutrition and athletic performance." *Journal of the American Dietetic Association* 100 (2001): 1543–1556.

Websites

GENERAL NUTRITION

American Dietetic Association
www.eatright.org

Americans' Food and Nutrition Attitudes and Behaviors
www.eatright.org/pr/2000/010300a.html

Dietary Guidelines
www.nal.usda.gov/fnic/dga/index.html

Dietary Reference Intakes
www.nap.edu

Dietary Supplements
www.nutrition.gov

Food Guide Pyramid
www.nal.usda.gov/fnic/Fpyr/pyramid.html

Food Labeling
www.cfsan.fda.gov

Healthy Eating Index
www.usda.gov/cnpp

Nutrient Content of Foods Using the Nutrient database
for Standard Reference
www.nal.usda.gov

Protein-Energy Malnutrition
www.who.int

EATING DISORDERS

Organizations providing guidance on eating disorders:
American Anorexia/Bulimia Association (AABA)
www.aabaphila.org

Harvard Eating Disorders Center
www.hedc.org

National Association for Anorexia Nervosa and Associated Disorders
(ANAD)
www.anad.org

Information on treating eating disorders:
IAEDP—International Association of Eating Disorders Professionals
www.iaedp.com

National Eating Disorder Association Information and Referral Program
www.nationaleatingdisorders.org

National Institute of Mental Health
www.nimh.gov

NEDSP—National Eating Disorders Screening Program
www.mentalhealthscreening.org/eat.htm

Support Groups:
Overeaters Anonymous Headquarters
www.overeatersanonymous.org

Vitality Inc.
www.tiac.net/users/vtlty

NUTRITION AND EXERCISE
Canada's physical activity guide
www.hc-sc.gc.ca/hppb/paguide

Typical activity patterns
www.ilsi.org/nhppress.html#2

WEIGHT MANAGEMENT
Financial costs of obesity
www.rand.org/publications/RB/RB4549

Obesity treatment guidelines
www.nhlbi.nih.gov/guidelines/obesity/ob_home.htm

Statistics related to body weight
www.cdc.gov/nchs/releases/02news/obesityonrise.htm

Weight Control Information Network
www.niddk.nih.gov/health/nutrit/pubs/statobes.htm

NUTRITION, HEALTH, AND DISEASE
American Cancer Society
www2.cancer.org

American Heart Association
www.americanheart.org

Fight Bac!
www.fightbac.org

Food Safety
www.foodsafety.gov

Websites

Healthy People 2010
www.health.gov/healthypeople

National Center for Health Statistics
www.cdc.gov/nchs

National Cholesterol Education Program
www.nhlbi.nih.gov/chd

Index

Index

Index

DRIs, 138
need, 23, 25, 38, 125–128, 135, 149
production, 147
sources, 21–22, 31, 39, 126–127, 150

Macronutrients, 26, 149
distribution ranges, 138
Malnutrition, 29, 39, 70, 90–91, 149
Metabolism, 23, 149
Micronutrients, 26, 149
Minerals, 22, 27, 112
DRIs, 141
need, 25–27, 29, 39, 125, 135, 149
sources, 21, 23, 128–130
UL, 143–144
Morbid obesity. *See* Extreme obesity
Mucus, 23, 149

Natural leanness, 70
Neurotransmitter, 14, 43, 111, 149
Night-eating syndrome, 109–111, 120, 149
Nutrient density, 126, 149
Nutrients, 149
absorption, 14, 23, 25, 39, 100
classes, 25–27, 39
deficiencies, 21, 29, 39, 86
digestion of, 13-14, 23, 25, 130
function, 21–23
needs, 24, 28–29, 31, 33, 39, 103, 119, 126, 130, 148, 150
sources, 14, 20–21, 30-36, 90, 128–129
uses, 23–24, 27
Nutrition, 1, 14, 20, 39, 150
education, 21, 103
good, 58, 90, 115
problems, 20, 83

Obesity, 29, 44, 51–52, 57, 73, 80, 150
discrimination, 69–70, 110
fear, 94, 97, 100, 103, 111–113, 116
gene, 72
health risks, 63, 68, 74, 109–110, 114
treatment, 107
Obesity epidemic, 68
Organic molecules, 27, 150
Overnutrition, 17, 29, 150
Overweight, 16–17, 45, 60, 63, 113, 150
and eating disorders, 107, 109, 120
discrimination, 69–70, 110
health risks of, 63, 65, 68–70, 72, 74

Pervasive refusal syndrome, 111, 113, 120
Phytochemical, 126, 130, 150
Prevention, eating disorders, 48–49
Protein, 26-27, 43, 72, 85
building blocks, 39, 147
DRIs, 138
enzymes, 148
need, 14, 23, 25–27, 125–128, 135, 149
sources, 21–22, 31, 128
Purging, 16–19, 79–81, 91, 150, *see also* Vomiting
behaviors, 92, 95–97, 99, 101–104, 107, 119–120
physical damage, 83, 94, 104

RDAs. *See* Recommended Dietary Allowances
Recommended Dietary Allowances (RDAs), 28–29, 147, 150

Satiety, 12–14, 43, 90, 101, 104, 150
Selective eating, 111, 113, 120

Picture Credits

page:

15: © Omni Photo Communications Inc./ Index Stock Imagery
24: Lambda Science Artwork
32: Courtesy USDA
33: Courtesy USDA
37: Courtesy USDA
51: Courtesy of Gary Koellhoffer
54: (left) © Underwood&Underwood/ CORBIS
54: (right) © Bettmann/CORBIS

56: (a) © Bettmann/CORBIS
56: (b) © Bettmann/CORBIS
64: AP Graphics
66: (left) © Frank Siteman/ Index Stock Imagery
66: (right) © Jim Perkins
69: © Jim Perkins
84: © Ed Quinn/CORBIS
115: © Allen Kennedy/CORBIS

Frontis 1: Agricultural Research Service, photo by Peggy Greb
Frontis 2: Agricultural Research Service, photo by Scott Bauer

Zyprexa is a trademark of Eli Lilly and Company Corp.